Beyond the Burning: Life and Death of the Ghetto

Beyond the Burning: Life and Death of the Ghetto

By STERLING TUCKER

What white Americans have never fully understood—but what the Negro American can never forget—is that white society is deeply implicated in the ghetto. White institutions created it, white institutions maintain it, and white society condones it.

—*National Advisory Commission on Civil Disorders*

NEW YORK ASSOCIATION PRESS

BEYOND THE BURNING: LIFE AND DEATH OF THE GHETTO

ASSOCIATION PRESS, 291 Broadway, New York, New York 10007

This is to acknowledge, with deep appreciation the professional assistance rendered to me by Linda Finkelstein, my editorial associate, and Carol Randles, my research assistant.

Thanks also to other staff associates and friends for helpful suggestions and other services.

First Printing 1968
Second Printing, 1969
Third Printing, 1970

To Alloyce, Michele, and Lauren.

Publisher's stock number: 1703 p., paper; 1963, cloth.
LIBRARY OF CONGRESS CATALOG CARD NUMBER: *68-9310*

PRINTED IN THE UNITED STATES OF AMERICA

Contents

INTRODUCTION BY THE AUTHOR 7

1. THE GHETTO TODAY 13
Ghetto walls are real . . . Progress—for somebody else . . . Housing needs become more acute . . . Exploitation in the name of law . . . A tax on being black . . . No welcome outside.

2. WHITE SUPREMACY, BLACK DESPERATION 36
Caught up in a system . . . To struggle or to submit? . . . Freed only to be re-enslaved . . . The charisma of black power.

3. IS THE BLACK GHETTO UNIQUE? 53
A tyranny of body and soul . . . Black *is* different . . . Comparison with other groups is not valid.

4. THE PERPETUATION OF THE GHETTO 69
What is progress? . . . ". . . A man with a job" . . . Not just brick and mortar . . . Education—sterilityville.

5. BLACK POWER FOR THE GHETTO 104
The only viable solution . . . Management and decentralization . . . Employment . . . A share in the profits . . . Equal opportunity versus equal results.

6. ELIMINATION OF THE GHETTO 123
Participation at all levels . . . A full stake in American society . . . Redistribution of population . . . Communication is the key.

7. AFTER THE FIRE 139
How will the Negro use his power? . . . Need for continuing reappraisal . . . Dilemma of the Church and the white liberal . . . Government must reassess.

NOTES 152

Dream Deferred

What happens to a dream deferred?

Does it dry up
like a raisin in the sun?
Or fester like a sore—
And then run?
Does it stink like rotten meat?
Or crust and sugar over—
like a syrupy sweet?
Maybe it just sags
like a heavy load.

Or does it explode?

—LANGSTON HUGHES

Introduction

When Gabriel Pope threw that first empty pop bottle at Sergeant Rankin's squad car—Wednesday, August 11, 1965, Watts, California—he symbolically unleashed centuries of pent-up animosity. Aiming his tortured fury at an embodiment of white oppression—the white cop in black man's territory—he began a senseless, but premeditated six days of violence.

Or so the story goes.

But was it Gabriel Pope who triggered the action, or did the white police when they arrested Marquette Frye for drunken driving or when they arrested Marquette's brother and mother whose only crime was coming to his defense?

Was the violence senseless? Were the Negroes foolishly lashing out at themselves by burning out their homes and further charring their lives, or were they consciously destroying that part of themselves that was the most repugnant, the most degrading, the most shameful, a ghetto with which they were no longer going to identify, whatever the cost?

Was the violence really premeditated and staged, or is it conceivable that groups of individuals, themselves the time-worn objects of oppression and injustice, will one day refuse to witness passively the meting out of more brutal injustice?

As Watts smoldered and Newark and Detroit burned, America entered a new era. The issue is no longer Negro versus white. Nor is it how to improve the life of the Negro or how to deal with the Negro problem. The people throwing the fire bombs now are not concerned with how many jobs the white man puts into the ghetto. They are not saying, "Give us better housing or we'll throw a bomb." When they demonstrate, they don't want the white man to give them anything. They simply want to throw a fire bomb. They want to tell society in their own way that it has placed a low premium on life in the ghetto, and the little bit of life left there they are willing to destroy to make America come to its senses.

There are a lot of people outside the ghetto who hear what the rioters are saying. But on Capitol Hill they don't. Most Congressmen continue to read their mail, and people who riot don't write in. City Hall doesn't want to hear them; the Establishment doesn't exactly like their style. Their actions and words are vulgar and iconoclastic, and in this country, officials don't like vulgarity while they revere tradition. Officialdom, therefore, reacts by tuning out, evidencing more of the let's-keep-the-invisible-men-invisible mentality. Is this not how America's leaders—indeed, America's middle classes—have reacted for decades? When the actions of others fall outside our sterile, rigid middle-class value system, we react by rejecting the perpetuators of those acts. They continue to reject our values and we further alienate them. So the cycle has gone.

No longer, however, for the rioters have broken through. They are prepared to blow up what won't be taken down and replaced.

While the reverberations of Gabriel Pope's pop bottle may still be sounding in our nation's streets, those streets have changed a great deal in the three short years since Watts bellowed its first warning. Cities and towns, North and South, those with a history of strained and abrasive race relations, those with years of outward racial peace, have all experienced—or live in fear of experiencing—violence in their streets. There is uncertainty and instability in communities in every section of the nation. Power structures have been unnerved, their actions and reactions belying the apparent calm and confidence which characterized past city administrations. Politicians no longer know how to assess what is politically expedient. White suburbanites don't know where to seek sanctuary; "liberal" organizations don't know how to react to the new sets of unorthodox signals.

But what is most distressing, most agonizingly real, is that no one is exempt from the fears, the misgivings and the guilt. In 1965 we could all point to Watts, the best of our numbers cursing the powers that created such a deprived and despairing population. And in concentrating our vision and criticism on the cruel misdeeds of others, we attempted to shut out our own insensitive acts, our own lethargy. In accusing others, we condoned ourselves; however bad *we* were, there were others who were worse. "It can't happen here" was the cry of the day. *Our* city is different!

But in 1968, the question is where *can't* it happen? What city is different? Youngstown, Washington, Kansas City, Trenton, Jackson, Detroit, Wilmington, Buffalo, Pampano Beach, Columbia, Cincinnati, Pittsburgh, Newark, Brooklyn, Chattanooga, Los Angeles. What city *is* different?

Three years ago seasonal distinctions were clear and only one time of year was to be feared, summer. Not so today, for summer has stretched back into early spring. Cities, we've learned, can seethe and erupt even under a cool sun.

Yet somehow, despite the intensification in feelings and actions, despite the uneasiness and national instability, the entire fabric of American life has not changed. Remaining constant throughout the upheaval is the country's stubborn unwillingness to focus on the real problems of the decade, its inability to face up to the causes of the upheaval. When the Establishment's own Commission on Civil Disorders issued its documented report, the country's leaders hardly acknowledged the stark findings and the sanguine recommendations. In a business-as-usual atmosphere, the country all but forgot the Commission's shocking discoveries a month after they were presented to the public. Even after the brutal and ugly assassination of Dr. Martin Luther King, Jr., and many tributes and kind gestures, the country went right back to praising nonviolence while it cursed those who continued to act out their bitterness. Little effort was made at understanding. No real effort was made at change.

Over a century ago, Abraham Lincoln met the challenge of his day. He freed the slave and thereby saved the Union. The challenge Americans face today is no less acute; nor are the decisions we must make any more difficult. We must free the black man and in so doing save our cities. The problem can no longer be viewed as a problem of survival for one particular group of people, but rather, it is a question of the survival of life itself. For rioting has truly become a tool of civil rights—not of civil rights leadership, not of most civil rights organizations. But directions are no longer being determined by the leadership of established organizations. Plays are being called by individuals and small groups who at some point in time take on leadership roles to find there are many who are willing to follow, many who are willing to die.

It is not just for civil rights leaders to go into the ghetto and reason with the discontented and offer more false hopes, tin promises. Their role is reasoning with legislators, for it is Congress and state house officials who decide the plight of American cities and their inhabitants. *They* are the real absentee landlords who drain the life and the spirit out of the ghetto.

We are faced with only two alternatives: either we decide to eliminate the ghettos ourselves, or they will be eliminated for us. We no longer have the luxury of a third choice.

Eliminating the ghetto is no longer synonymous with cleaning up and painting. For all too long we've tried to whitewash our problems by painting over them. Most of the riots, Detroit's and New Haven's especially, were signals that a patch-up approach is about as unacceptable as no approach at all, given no commitment to root out the basic causes of the decay.

There was a time when new programs aimed at ameliorating one aspect of one problem in the ghetto were greeted with wild enthusiasm. Not so 1967-68. When the Urban Convocation called for the creation of two million new jobs in the late summer of 1967, nobody even got excited. Programs alone don't arouse the ghetto any longer because people know they will not eliminate the problem. Nothing less than a new national state of mind is acceptable. The ghetto dweller wants an equal chance to make it, an equal chance to walk in daylight, an equal chance to be heard. He is looking for the recognition of the dignity of every man.

Elimination of the ghetto means construction of a major blueprint for a mass overhauling of the ghetto area. It means giving up vested interests for the provision of a new organization of industry, training and education. It means white America sacrificing short-range advantage for long-range survival. And it means money—lots of it. In short, it means discarding old approaches and old masters for revolutionary thinking and action.

Eliminating the ghetto also means transitional years, years devoted to planning and construction while the ghetto remains physically intact and old patterns of segregation persist. During this period, discrimination could, in large part, be wiped out, were the management of the ghetto but turned over to the people who live there. If black men were allowed to run their own lives, manage their own businesses, be their own landlords, they would not face daily degradation and dehumanization. The foundation of the whole ghetto mentality would begin to crumble and the transitional months and years would be tolerable enough so that riots and widespread destruction would probably be precluded.

It is during this transitional period that remedial programs, self-help, and training programs are palatable. Such programs could never be offered as ends in themselves, but within the larger framework they would be both workable and helpful. At best, they could improve the present while society was working toward long-range solutions.

There is no question but that the proposed would be a monumental undertaking, even for the most humane of nations. Given a society that makes a god of the status quo, a society which has institutionalized discrimination, it seems unrealistic, idealistic, politically inexpedient.

And, indeed, it is all those things. Yet the money is available —we daily have spent over sixty million dollars to save South Vietnam from something. The manpower can be recruited—about five hundred thousand men were sent to Vietnam. All we need is the will.

Dr. King tried to inspire the nation to develop that will. He did not succeed.

If a man with Dr. King's sincerity, integrity and humanity could not—in his life or through his death—bring a confused and callous nation to its senses, there seems little that individual men can do. And the most a book can do is to attempt to increase the nation's understanding of the depth of the problem. It might help a troubled nation understand how it got to be in the dangerous position in which it now finds itself. It can also offer some routes of escape. Would that it could redirect the traffic.

This book sets out to examine the metropolitan problems which produce tension, affliction and rioting and which deny equal access and opportunity to the American Negro. It will argue that any steps short of ghetto elimination are doomed because it is the ghetto and its perpetrators which force man to live in a perpetual state of desperation. It is the ghetto which breeds violence.

The book will further argue that if America agrees to undertake the long process of eliminating ghettos, it must at the same time place the mangement of the ghetto in the hands of the area residents. Immediate rewards are needed. The poor know better than most that "the Government has become attuned to falsehood as a routine way of conducting its affairs, to the point where hardly a day passes without producing its own challenge to creduality."[1] The poor will no longer believe or even listen patiently to promises.

Long-range programs will be offered to achieve the first goal—ghetto elimination—while short-range steps will be advanced to make the second—increased black management—possible and palatable.

The book will also examine the dilemmas faced by black leaders, black people, white liberals, the Church and the government, pointing out that a society in the midst of rebellion, with revolution threatening, forces at least a reexamination of old roles and at most a shift in leadership, emphasis, degree of commitment and tactics.

Many will wish that less had been written about the problem and that more had been offered in the way of solutions. They will claim that they know what the problems are; if only someone could suggest a way to solve them.

The author is convinced that it is not solutions America lacks. A great deal has been written about the problems, it is true, but just as much has been written about how to attack them. What America lacks is the will to put into operation the solutions it has already found. It still balks when it sees the price tag; it is not yet ready to reorder its priorities.

Consequently, the problem of the Negro and the problem of the city must be stated over and over again until they, in fact, become the two principal items on America's agenda. As long as they are relegated to secondary status, it matters little what solutions are offered, for they have no chance of being implemented.

1

The Ghetto Today

> You are still in jail, in the hole or out of the hole. You are in jail in the street or behind bars. It is the same thing, a matter of existing. . . .[1]
>
> —ARTHUR DUNMEYER

At a current affairs seminar held on a college campus, the general area of concern was the Negro ghetto. Conversation seemed to flow easily between black and white participant until a white college freshman asked whether there really were walls around Harlem. The whites who shared the room were discomforted by the coed's question and were quick to censure her for naïveté—indeed, her embarrassing ignorance. Their "noes" reverberated. There followed a minute or two of awkward silence, for the black bodies—in direct contrast—were still, unagitated, serene. A few faces betrayed slight amusement. None would dare to answer that question so unequivocally.

There was something apocryphal in the uncalculating and inoffensive probings of the young mind. The innocent, fearlessly curious, often remind the more life-weary of the deeper truths of man's existence. They mouth what the rest refuse to consider and often cause or force painful recognition. The question posed that evening haunted all in the room.

GHETTO WALLS ARE REAL

It haunts me still, for ghetto walls exist not only in the minds of the naïve. They are no mere creation of fantasy. Though they are invisible, they not only exist—they also define and circumscribe the lives of those within their confines. They are a living force which daily affects the thinking, the decisions, and the actions of those inside. An actual wall could be no more threatening, no more oppressive, than the nonvisible wall, the noose, surrounding and choking each American ghetto, each inhabitant of each American ghetto.

The ghetto places a peculiar brand of chains on the feet of its inhabitants. To the outsider, the chains appear long enough to allow extraordinary mobility, but, in fact, they tear away at the flesh of him whose strides are too long, whose steps are too quick, whose destination is the other side of the wall. The outsider assures himself that the chains are virtually weightless, and when he tries them for size, indeed they are. Yet, on the foot of the ghetto dweller the chains are weighty, for they can't be fastened and unfastened by an act of will. The longer they're worn, the more they oppress. The longer they cling, the heavier they feel, the deeper they scar. They hold back the child who reaches for only some of the skeleton joys of childhood; they overpower the student who fights for an education; they cripple the man in the race for a job.

Most ghetto residents learn to adjust to a life in chains. Some choose to give up when their bodies start to ache; others fight until the hurt and the pain subdue them; only a few choose to suffer endless torment for uncertain goals.

There is little in the ghetto world that offers hope or provides solace. Its walls shut out even the dream of escape. Its chains make a mockery of freedom. Its buildings, its grounds, its stores, its schools offer nothing of beauty, little of worth.

The ghetto house is a hovel or a shack, rarely a cheerful, warm home. It is often unpainted; opaque boards may serve as windows. The wood is dry and shows evidence of rotting. Most houses on a given street look similar. The eye quickly tires of the colorless study in monotony.

Around the houses and the tenement buildings are miles of cold, grey concrete. Grass and trees are a luxury which residents cannot afford to purchase, which society is not ready to provide. The only green the observer can find are straggly weeds that sprout in the dirt. And even this sign of life gets buried beneath the feet of active youth who have a choice between the mud yard and the concrete streets for their games.

The inside of the ghetto house, though often clean and neat, surpasses the outdoors in its dingy appearance, for light doesn't easily penetrate the cardboard or wood in the windows, and the kerosene lamps give off little glow. Unpainted walls make the rooms appear cold and austere. Rotted, creaking floors and peeling ceilings add the finishing stroke to the picture of bleakness.

Rats are permanent tenants of the dwellings, no matter how clean and neat the individual home, apartment, or room. A person could polish and scrub his piece of soil forever and the rats would return, finding the lure of the nearby junk yard, the uncollected garbage and the dilapidation hard to resist.

Most floors are bare, the linoleum half on, half worn off. Carpeting is a symbol of luxury, whatever its condition; when it appears, it is a pathetic sight—worn out, uneven, faded from age and usage.

Heat is often provided by a coal stove expected to heat three or four rooms, but which can barely warm one on cold nights. In winter's deep freezes, families cuddle together; babies are bundled up in layers of old clothes until they can barely move.

The appliances that are provided or purchased are in poor working order. In addition, their wiring is often inadequate. The faulty wiring and the dry wood of the house combine to make fire an ever-present threat.

Noise is the perennial companion of the ghetto resident. There are simply too many bodies crammed into too little space for quiet to prevail. Indeed, the ghetto dweller is so accustomed to noise that silence seems ominous. He who seeks serenity or calm must wait until three or four in the morning.

PROGRESS—FOR SOMEBODY ELSE

The ghetto resident suffers from other insecurities which are of a vastly different nature. There was a time when, as bad as ghetto conditions were, the man in the ghetto could always count on a place to lay his head. The ghetto belonged to him, even though he didn't own or control it. This is the case no longer, for his neighborhood is being chopped up by public works programs.

Unjustly, unreasonably, discriminatorily, the country has opted to build most of its freeways on the poor man's back. Industry isn't built in ghetto communities. Cultural centers don't sprout up on the ghetto's fertile soil. The projects that are built in these areas are designed not to infuse downtrodden areas with new life and vitality. Rather, they are designed to clear away existing housing to clear out ghetto residents, to decrease the acreage of the black neighborhood, and to exacerbate the overcrowding problem the ghetto Negro already faces.

The ghetto dweller might not mind so much if the freeways were for his use. But programs imposed on the ghetto are usually not for the ghetto but for those who pass through. Highways never benefit those too poor to own a car.

And as though that weren't enough, urban renewal projects either shrink his domain or cause it to disappear completely. The bulldozer steals his tarnishing crown and gives it to the middle-class family which already has more than its fair share of houses and land. Everyone in the ghetto suffers as a result, especially the aged. I once visited an elderly lady and four of her grandchildren in a section of Northwest Washington that was on the calendar of destruction. I remember how she cried because she was going to have to move from the only home she ever remembered, from the only home she had ever owned. Her husband had been dead for many years, and her sole income came from day work. She knew she would never be granted a loan for another house because her income was so meagre; and even if some establishment agreed to a loan, she knew the interest rates would be far out of reach, and the mortgage would be larger than she could afford over a period much longer than a woman at her age could take on.

Urban renewal projects are also responsible for killing off communities years before their time. When demolition begins, completion dates may still be years away. In the interim, deterioration sets in in neighborhoods that are still inhabited. The city lessens services or calls them to a halt; officialdom looks away. In the Pierce Street section of Washington, D.C., a full month before the area had to be completely cleared of inhabitants we found that the Police Department was unaware that anyone was still living on the street. Water gushing from mains often flooded the streets. Rats increased in numbers and could even be seen in daylight feeding on trash dumped on the sidewalk by passersby—the trash that had been forgotten by the Sanitation Department.

Looters, goaded on by junk dealers and second-hand merchants, often find their way into the unoccupied homes and gut them of all fixtures—sinks, commodes, tiles, light bulbs, even pipes. An eighty-year-old man was one of the last persons left living in the Pierce Street area. One night he was awakened by a group of vandals who, thinking his house had been deserted like the rest, began their marauding.

The eighty-year-old man and a family with six children were the only people left on deserted Pierce Street in the middle of June 1966. The deadline for vacating the street had been June 1, but the old man's folder with a priority application for public housing had been lost somewhere downtown. And there was no unit available for the family which was forced to await the completion of a new development.

Is it any wonder that people panic and flee from renewal areas months before they need to leave, falling victim to those out to exploit them? They feel the need to act immediately, for they are afraid and they are desperate. I recall a woman in Northwest Washington who had decided to remain in her house until the deadline. The two houses adjoined to hers were vacant, but she understood that the Redevelopment Land Agency had agreed not to move bulldozers in until all inhabitants had moved out. Consequently, she felt secure in remaining. One morning she awoke suddenly, feeling her house shaking beneath her. A bulldozer had attacked an adjoining house which within hours was rubble. Her outside walls were loosened in the process, plaster covered her floors, and in that evening's heavy rain she lacked protection from the weather. Though the relocation plan had said that she didn't have to move yet, the bulldozer proclaimed that she did.

When blocks of ghetto dwellings are razed and neighborhoods disappear, inhabitants have no place to go but to other already swarming hives. Overcrowding is the result. Two families whose homes were to be torn down in Washington's Southwest area were promised adequate housing by renewal authorities. But when the bulldozers came, no housing had been provided. One family—a mother, father and seven children—moved into a three-bedroom house in Northwest Washington as did an eighth child with her three children. The second family, a mother and her fifteen children, could not afford to rent a house. The woman was forced to rent and share a four-bedroom house with three of her other daughters who brought a total of twelve more children in the home.

Overcrowding viciously destroys families, for it intensifies problems by making privacy impossible. Husband and wife have no time alone. They share their bedroom or the living room with several youngsters each night. In some homes this means that ordinary marital disagreements and marital joys are engaged in quietly, hurriedly, or surreptitiously if at all, and always fearfully, for a child might be awake or might awaken. In other homes, parents resign themselves to an impossible situation and stop trying to muffle and hide what young ears will hear anyway, what curious eyes will manage to see. They know their acts cause early experimentation and a permissive attitude toward sex and morality, but there is nothing they feel they can do in these circumstances to stem the tide.

Children share rooms and beds with one another and must run to the street, break away from home, for a moment alone. Often there are not enough places around the table for the entire family, so the family splits and eats dinner in shifts. For students there is no quiet place to study; for adolescents there is no place for courtship. I can vividly remember talking with a teenage girl who summarized the pathos of her oppressed generation in a tale she reluctantly told. A week before we spoke, her boyfriend had brought her home from a date and asked if he might step inside to say goodnight. He had forgotten where he was. Somewhat saddened and deeply humiliated, she tearfully reminded him, "We live in one room, remember, we live in one room."

Life presses in—humanity cries to burst out. It cannot be surprising that so many escape to the street and prefer the world outside where breathing is a little easier.

HOUSING NEEDS BECOME MORE ACUTE

As urban renewal and other federal programs cause further impaction in ghetto areas, housing needs grow. Demand exceeds supply and the buying power of the ghetto dollar decreases.

The man most victimized by this system is the man who is poor and black and the father of many. He faces all the handicaps of his brothers and then some. There was a time when each city had numbers of large homes which could accommodate big families. Such structures are now used as libraries or halls, if they haven't been sacrificed to the god, urban renewal. The few large dwellings which remain on the housing market are in great demand, despite the fact that many have been turned into tenements, despite the fact that zoning officials have made it possible for ruthless landlords to exploit the poor by allowing them to cut up these large houses into small apartments without adding additional facilities. Owners find they can often set whatever limitations they want on their property and the homes will still never be vacant. Consequently, some restrict even the large units to families with few or no children, reasoning that the smaller the number of occupants, the fewer the number of repairs. What is left for the protector of the large family is the most run-down dwelling with an exorbitant price tag. So the man whose every waking and sleeping hour is plagued by the vision of open, hungry mouths is the same man who is expected to pay dearly for dilapidated shelter. The Department of Public Welfare in the District of Columbia found that some large families could find no housing to accommodate them.

> We found some who had already accepted separation as a partial answer. Other families were on the verge of breaking up where it appeared that it would no longer be possible to maintain a common home.[2]

How hard it must be for such individuals not to be antagonistic to the causes of their problems! How ruthless and cruel a system which can cause such great oppression, such pervasive depression.

Manning the controls and preserving this near feudal system is the absentee landlord who, more often than not, hides from his guilt in padded suburban splendor. He gets his power and the freedom to exploit from legislators who refuse to pass rent control measures; each bureau of licenses and inspections sits as a silent jury and frequently sanctions his misdeeds; police protection is provided by the courts which also act as collection agents.

The whole system works to further oppress the ghetto. It increases the power of the strong while it debilitates the weak. There are seldom any checks and balances; scales of justice be damned! In most run-down areas of Washington, D.C., landlords charge tenants a six- or seven-dollar fee if their monthly rent is received late. Account isn't taken of the past payment record of the tenant; it doesn't matter if the rent is but a day or two late. Most slum landlords in Washington refuse to grant leases to tenants. If their hand is forced, some will reluctantly agree to a thirty-day lease or even to a longer one providing it contains a clause which grants the landlord the power to evict for almost any reason. The tenant is left unprotected. The landlord has all the authority and he uses it. In 1963, there were 92,000 evictions in Washington, D.C., alone.[3]

Using the threat or the actuality of eviction, the landlord keeps his tenants in line. Retaliatory eviction of a tenant who reports Housing Code violations to authorities is a common practice. In 1963 a number of families living in a run-down apartment house on Girard Street in the District of Columbia signed a petition listing Code violations in their building and presented it to the Bureau of Licenses and Inspection. The violations were numerous, ranging from a coal furnace in such poor repair that the building went for days without heat to unlit hallways and stopped-up plumbing. The man who drew up the petition and whose name appeared first among the signatories received an eviction notice shortly after the Bureau received the petition. The Housing authorities had actually given the petition *with the names of the complainants attached* to the landlord. Since it was cheaper and easier to evict than to make the needed repairs, the landlord chose to evict.

Tenants find it almost impossible to get repairs made. In the Shaw area of Washington a woman stays up each night to keep the rats away from her children and her new-born baby. She is not atypical. Each time she attempts to fill the rat holes herself, the rats knock them out again. Complaints to the landlord's office have been met by unfulfilled promises or with claims that the person in charge is out of the office.

Rents in slum areas are exorbitant. As far back as 1963 a one-bedroom apartment could rarely be found in Washington for less than seventy-five to eighty-five dollars a month *excluding* utilities. It is interesting that in almost all of Washington's slum buildings, utilities are not included in the rent. This is because utilities are so very expensive in run-down dwellings. In an apartment with numerous cracks and holes in the walls and roof, heat costs dearly as it must warm the outdoor air as well as the air inside. In addition, the furnaces are often in such poor state that they need to be turned way up and, even then, the oven is usually left on on cold nights. It is not uncommon to find that ghetto dwellers pay as much for utilities as they do for rent in winter months.

Most measures proposed to protect the poor are either summarily rejected or subverted by the ruling monarchs and the politicians who support them. For example, as of March 1967 rent control laws were operant in only one major American city, New York.[4] Yet, the existence of rent control laws could make life livable for the poor—witness the law in New York State which grants the State Rent Commissioner the power to reduce rents where deterioration, poor services, and hazardous conditions prevail.

The absence of rent control gives landlords a frightening amount of autonomy. As the housing supply shrinks, these men can, and do, raise rents mercilessly, knowing full well that their subjects have no option but to pay, for they have no place else to go. Such a system encourages greed and man is rewarded for his inhumanity to man.

EXPLOITATION IN THE NAME OF LAW

Further menacing the life of the ghetto are the bureaus of licenses and inspections referred to briefly above. Bureaus of licenses and inspections were established to *protect* the tenant. On paper these governmental units have the power to use sanctions against landlords who do not keep their properties in safe, sound, and sanitary condition. Their potential for uplifting cities is tremendous as Hubert Humphrey saw:

> If you gave out as many tickets to the landlord who breaks the housing laws as you do to the fellow who drives downtown and overparks, you'd have a different kind of city.[5]

Yet, in practice, most license and inspection bureaus work in collusion with the ruling elite and oppress the very people they are asked to save from oppression. According to Dr. Sox, Director of Public Health in San Francisco:

The slums of our cities were not created by the occupants, but by the failure of code enforcement agencies to provide strict and consistent enforcement.[6]

In Washington, D.C., the Department of Licenses and Inspections has undermined rather than enforced the Housing Code by allowing—indeed encouraging—delays in correcting Code violations. According to a publication of the Girard Street Association[7] printed in 1963:

Inspections of apartment buildings are conducted only once in two years (for license purposes). If a violation is found the offending landlord knows that by various extensions of deadlines, appeals and excuses, he can postpone repairs for another year and a half. If after all that time he still has not corrected the violation, even then nothing happens to him. His case is referred to the Corporation Counsel, the public prosecutor for the District of Columbia. He is then granted another hearing and given another three months extension, and, if his excuses are good enough, he may be given yet another one.
Only if he neglects to begin his repairs by the time this second extension runs out is the landlord brought to trial for the criminal offense of negligence. If he loses in court, the worst that can happen to him is a $300 fine or 10 days in jail, and up to the day of writing no landlord has ever served a jail sentence for breaking the D.C. Housing Code.[8]

Up to the date of this writing, no landlord has yet served a sentence for violation of the Code in Washington; and while some of the procedures described above may have been changed by the new chief who recently revitalized the Department, the manner in which governmental agencies deal with ghetto residents in most parts of the country is accurately characterized.

Tenants have often tried to force the Department of Licenses and Inspections to act by issuing complaints, but to no avail. Neighborhood workers in the Urban League's Neighborhood Center in the District report oft-repeated instances in which a renter requests the Department to inspect his dwelling and issue a complaint. In some cases, no complaint is ever registered. In others the rent increases or the tenant is evicted, thanks to a curious leakage of information. In each instance, improvements are not made. If, on the other hand, the ghetto dweller owns his home, workers report that L and I officials are a little too anxious to demand improvements.

Perhaps the attitude of such bureaus was best typified in Washington in 1967 when a campaign was announced by the Corporation Counsel's office to force landlords to improve the maintenance of their property. The government had uncovered recurring violations and was ready to launch an intensive inspection program. It planned to haul into court those landlords who were in violation of the building codes and the regulations of the government of the District of Columbia. In the early weeks of the campaign, the Department of Licenses and Inspections attempted to sabotage the operation by turning over to the Corporation Counsel cases containing insufficient information and cases with violations too petty to merit prosecution. A memorandum issued by the Department's Housing Division termed the campaign "discriminatory" and stated that an attempt to single out property owners with large holdings and many violations would ". . . completely emasculate our code enforcement programs." The Department chief admitted that he felt special consideration needed to be given to large holders of slum property because their rate of repair was so high. He further claimed that his office would not engage in any campaign aimed specifically at slum landlords.[9]

Courts have remained the enemy of the poor because they have traditionally taken the side of the landlord in landlord-tenant cases. Judges, in all too many instances, automatically assume the tenant guilty. All a landlord need do is appear and file eviction charges against a tenant who may be paying 50 per cent of his income for rent. The problems the tenant faces are rarely taken into account by the law or by the interpreter of the law. There is no concern about how exorbitant the rent might be. There is no concern about the condition of the housing. If the rent hasn't been paid, the defendant is automatically adjudged guilty. This is why hundreds of cases are cranked through daily, the routinized cadence of the proceedings carrying itself along, as though self-propelled, deadening interest, life and hope, and smacking of all that is dispassionate and removed. Praised is the magistrate who can further accelerate the machinery; opprobrium is reserved for that defendant who questions or challenges and thereby impedes progress. What a strange perversion of values when efficiency seems more honored than justice in a court of law.

Officials haven't yet learned that law untempered with mercy breeds contempt of the law—not respect for it. It is little wonder that ghetto residents do not always hold the law in esteem; they have been the victims of more uneven justice than any other segment of society. They have seen too much exploitation in the name of the law. They rarely see laws operating in their interest or for their protection. What they do see is an abundance of laws operating to control and exploit them.

Further jeopardizing the case of the poor is the fact that most city judges are middle class.

> They can easily mistake a certain manner of dress or speech, alien or repugnant to them but ordinary enough in the defendant's world, as an index of moral worthlessness. . . . They can mistake the defendant's resentment against the social evils with which he lives as evidence of criminality.[10]

As poor and crowded housing conditions poison family ties, so ghetto schools murder, for they kill off initiative, inquisitiveness, the will and the desire to learn. Ghetto schools are generally the most run-down, the oldest. In Washington, D.C., in 1967 the median age of the ghetto school was almost sixty years.[11] Books are very often handed down from other schools whose supply has been refurbished. In Washington three editions of the same text have been used at the same time in the same classroom. Tattered books are often held together with string. Supplies are generally short. Desks have deep scars and broken parts. Walls are replete with obscenities, halls are narrow and dingy. Broken windows make the weather outside very much a part of the classroom. Plumbing is in a poor state; showers often don't work. There is a paucity of organized gym activity because there is a scarcity of equipment. There may be but one basketball and a lone football for an entire junior or senior high. There is inadequate nursing service. Some schools are without a nurse for a full day or two every week. The per pupil expenditure is low. The average annual cost per pupil in the thirty-two districts surrounding Cleveland is $634, in Cleveland itself $418.[12] In Washington's predominantly Negro schools $292 were spent per elementary pupil in 1963-64.[13] Contrast this with the $460 spent in neighboring Montgomery County.

Almost everything in the school seems to discourage learning. Books are often not allowed to leave school—administrators fear they will not return. In some Washington schools children who lose a book cannot receive another until the lost book has been paid for. Library facilities are inadequate within the school and without; in Harlem there are but six libraries servicing a population of over 232,000. Many teachers are uninterested or disinterested in teaching. Rufus Mayfield, an unemployed free-lance consultant to the Washington Urban League and former chairman of the Board of Directors of Pride, Inc.,[14] claims that teachers instilled no desire to learn. They didn't even try to make lessons interesting, and

> . . . pretty soon you just say to hell with it. Why should we have to learn why George Washington crossed the Delaware or when Columbus discovered America? We're tired of being taught the past. Look at the white kids—they learn equations and stuff. They learn the future.

The teacher is often in the school against his will. Many whites are fearful and many Negroes are ashamed to teach inside the ghetto. Some teachers on tenure are given ghetto assignments when there is no other way to punish them for inappropriate behavior in a nonghetto classroom. A few take out on the students the hostility they feel for the system. Others just don't expect much of the young people. They give little and, therefore, don't receive much.

Many such schools resemble detention centers or reformatories because of the rigidity, inflexibility and emphasis on discipline. The administration reminds the teacher that the best classroom is the quiet classroom. School officials point out repeatedly that since the children are not going to produce much anyway, energy might just as well be expended in keeping the peace.

In the ghetto, large numbers of teachers are rated on the basis of how few students they send to the office. The result is that many will attempt to handle all student discipline problems within the classroom to the end of less teaching, more antagonism, increased hostility. The atmosphere in such a class is tense. The teacher is always on guard lest the students should get out of line and threaten his reputation. The students sense the teacher's antagonism and react in kind. Distrust abounds, as once again the ghetto youth is faced with the suspicious, uncaring adult. As the day-to-day drama unfolds, it is learning which gets sacrificed. Students are quick to see that apathy pays off and that questioning, curiosity, and excitement threaten. They learn their lessons quickly and by second or third grade understand the stakes. Most give in or give up.

Those youngsters who persist against all odds and do not drop out might well be termed "pushouts." They graduate, yes, but few along the way cared enough to stop them, to help them, to see them. Consequently, most are ill-prepared to meet what lies ahead. The youngsters emerging with academic credentials are the accidents, and not because there aren't many who have ability and potential.

When ghetto youths enter school, they are not far behind the national norms despite the educational impoverishment of their homes. But as they progress through the system, the disparity in performance between them and the non-slum youth increases. The average verbal achievement level of the third-grade Negro student in the Midwest is approximately one year behind that of the average white student. By twelfth grade, the difference is almost three years.[15] Studies done by the Civil Rights Commission in individual cities reveal that this is the normal pattern.[16]

The teacher in the ghetto cannot solve the problems of the ghetto. He cannot solve the problems of education. But he does have the opportunity to solve problems of individual spirits. He is given young minds which are suffering incomprehensible and debilitating agonies. As the teacher fails to teach ghetto youth that they are victims of the system, he teaches them that they are out of step with society. As he allows his classroom to mirror life, he convinces his students that they aren't bright, that they're inferior, that they're in school because the law requires them to be there. Most teachers have too much at stake to risk teaching that it is society which is insufficient, not the ghetto student. Consequently, the classroom becomes the fertile breeding ground for feelings of guilt and inferiority. It refuses to mourn even the death of dignity. It becomes a six-hour-a-day sentence, a place to which the student must return daily so that he can repeat a ritual according to the law.

A section of *The Little Prince* has some wisdom for the ghetto school. The reader may recall that the little prince visited an asteroid where he talked to the king. The king pointed out that all his subjects obey him, that he rules over all the universe, that even the stars are under his control. He states that everything does what he asks. The little prince is incredulous and asks why this is the case. How can a man's every request be granted? Because my requests are reasonable, replies the king.

> One must require from each one the duty which each can perform. . . . Accepted authority rests first of all on reason. If you ordered your people to go and throw themselves into the sea, they would rise up in revolution. I have the right to require obedience because my orders are reasonable.

Then to the prince, who asks him to order a sunset, the king replies,

> You shall have your sunset. I shall command it. But, according to my science of government, I shall wait until conditions are favorable.
>
> That will be about—about—that will be this evening about twenty minutes to eight.[17]

All too often, teachers in the ghetto expect, if not demand, that ghetto youth act like middle-class children. They expect them to respond to the same stimuli, conform to the same value system. Are such expectations evaluated in terms of their reasonableness? Rarely. Yet, when ghetto youth do not respond to the teachers' requests, it is the youth who are scrutinized and condemned—not the requests.

A TAX ON BEING BLACK

The shabby ghetto homes and the schools that teach despair have their parallels in other areas of ghetto life. Indeed, ghetto dwellers see only decay unless they venture forth outside the walls. *Decaying* or *inadequate* describes accurately everything from the barroom to the schoolroom, the alley to the park. *Decadent* describes accurately the absence of all that is cultural, the presence—the overabundance—of things that corrupt, the bar, the junkie, the pimp, the runner, the pawn shop, the fortune teller.

The ghetto store is one monument to graying mediocrity, uncaring neglect. Aisles are narrow, lighting is low-keyed, walls remain unpainted, attractive displays seem a contradiction in terms. Floors that aren't yellow from years of encrusted wax are gray from ground-in dirt. Merchandise is rarely encased; it is more often strewn about on worn tables, no pattern to the disorder. To establish a pattern would take time, and time costs money.

The ghetto store owner knows he need use little, if any, of his profit for improvements. He knows the ghetto is a captive market and learned early that business will prosper without the frills. So, the ghetto store is one more reminder to the ghetto dweller that he isn't worth much anyway, not even the cost of a few amenities. His kind are not entitled to a few of the niceties of life, not even from the man whose profit they insure.

People who live in the ghetto are also forced to pay more for less. As Adam Clayton Powell pointed out when testifying before Senator Ribicoff's Subcommittee on Executive Reorganization:

> They have to pay a tax on being black. It costs about 20 per cent or more to live in a black ghetto anyway. . . . a 1-day-old loaf of bread in Beverly Hills costs 10 cents and that same loaf of bread in Watts costs 22 cents, the same loaf of bread, 1 day old.[18]

According to *The Wall Street Journal:*

> A comparison between prices of a dozen items at two outlets of one store chain, one in Harlem and one in a white neighborhood of Manhattan, shows that Harlem shoppers must pay more for half of them.[19]

A supermarket chain in the riot area of Watts was found to charge an average of 3 per cent more than a Beverly Hills store in the same chain. A recent study by the Federal Trade Commission charged that a special brand of inflation plagues the Washington, D.C., ghetto resident. A portable television set selling in any department store for $129.95 would cost $249.95 in the "low-income market" store.[20] In Hough, prices go up on the tenth day of every month—Mother's Day, the day the Aid-to-Dependent-Children checks are received.

When the sharp cost of ghetto credit is added to the cost of goods that is already out of line, the final price tag can be staggering, often twice the retail price of the item. Those who make half as much are thus expected to pay a 200 per cent mark-up. In East Harlem, most stores maintain a "multi-price policy." The price of an individual item is determined by the shopkeeper's assessment of the shopper: Is he a poor risk? Is he naïve? Was he referred here by another merchant who must be paid a commission?

One Saturday a reporter and I worked out a scheme whereby I would get some firsthand information about ghetto store practices and his newspaper would print an article on the experience. I put on some old clotnes and walked in and out of Washington's Seventh Street stores, stores known for shoddy goods and sharp prices. Before entering a store, I looked at the merchandise in the window and in three instances hungry shopkeepers all but dragged me inside. The first thing I was asked was whether I worked for the Federal Government. At first, I assumed the shopkeepers wanted Federal employees as customers because they were good credit risks, but I later realized that they wanted nothing to do with government workers because government wages couldn't be garnished. And they didn't want customers who were good credit risks. They wanted people who weren't, people who would buy far more than they could afford.

I discovered another sharp practice which such merchants openly engage in. They sell a customer an item—a refrigerator, for instance. When payment on the refrigerator is almost completed, they encourage the same person to purchase a dining-room table, and near the end of that payment, convince him to buy a couch and so on. All purchases overlap. If at any time the customer defaults on a payment, a truck backs up to his door, a driver shoves some fine print in front of his face and takes back *all* of the merchandise, despite the fact that the first two or three or four items had been paid for many times over in terms of dollars.

Profit-seeking in its most malevolent form takes place in a well-known ghetto institution, the pawn shop. This enterprise can prosper only as its clients despair. Its business improves as the plight of its customers worsens. The pawn shop dealer encourages theft, for he will buy hot merchandise, no questions asked, and thus rewards the robber. Yet, caged-in pawn shops dot all ghettos, the compelling testimony of a plagued population. Pawn shops exist because there is a need for them. And there is a need for them in the ghetto, not because of the people who live there, but because of the set of circumstances faced by and imposed upon the people who live there. Pawn shops are a last resort, and they thrive in the ghetto precisely because people are so desperate that they will try anything—even a last resort.

The numbers racket is popular for similar reasons. People who don't have anything want to get something for nothing. The only way to beat the system is to turn two cents into five dollars, fifty cents into a thousand dollars. The few cents can't buy anything anyway, and operating within the system is possible for others, not for them.

The ghetto dweller is further victimized by the very services which the city should provide to serve and protect him. The police department, for one. In some major cities, a larger percentage of the police force operates in the ghetto than in other areas of the community. Yet the presence of the police does not represent police protection, as any ghetto dweller is quick to point out. When I lived in Canton, Ohio, a lady ran into the Urban League office one day and excitedly asked me to call the police because there was a disturbance in the neighborhood. I called, and while reporting the details, the voice at the other end boomed: "Those are just niggers down there. They're always fighting!" With that he hung up.

The white policeman is at least as unsympathetic to the problems of the black man as the rest of society. But his treatment of the black man is infinitely more harsh because he has direct authority that he can exercise, and he will usually be protected, even in the misuse of that authority. How many policemen have been found guilty of brutality to a ghetto resident? Very few. Yet, privately, the highest police authorities admit that they have great difficulty convincing members of their forces to act with constraint and compassion. Publicly, their denials ring loud and clear.

Anti-black feelings are strong in most police departments. According to the Reiss report, a study made for the National Crime Committee, 75 per cent of the white policemen who work in the predominantly black areas of Washington, Chicago, and Boston have "markedly prejudiced" attitudes toward Negroes. Only 1 per cent expressed attitudes sympathetic toward them.[21] Data from the same study suggests that in a city like Washington, D.C., with close to three thousand policemen, there are thousands of cases of physical abuse to Negroes every year and tens of thousands of cases of verbal abuse.[22]

Consequently, many ghetto youths are saying more and more that they don't want police protection any longer. They want protection from the police. Ghetto residents are tired of being looted en route to police stations. They have been manhandled enough. Their cries for help have too long gone unheeded. The white cop is their enemy and they mean to run him out of their land. As a thirty-three-year-old Harlem resident put it:

> The white cops, they have a damn sadistic nature. They are really a sadistic type of people and we, I mean me, myself, we don't need them here in Harlem. We don't need them! They don't do the neighborhood any good. . . . They start more violence than any other people start. They start violence, that's right.[23]

Yet many a policeman thinks he is accepted in the ghetto. He mistakes surface politeness for sincere concern and trust and fails to see the real emotions his uniform and his manners evoke. I sometimes ride with the police late at night in an attempt to see the problems they face and the way they handle them. One night I rode with a precinct captain and one of Washington's ex-commissioners. We stopped at a crowded fish-fry place and as we walked to the counter, the captain stopped at a few tables, fingering the shoulders of some of the customers, patting others on the back. He had enough smiles for all. "Hi, Mary; hello Sue; how ya' doing, John? Don't choke on the fish!" Later we barged into a few area houses for no apparent reason, and watched the captain walk in and out of rooms. Residents had no advance warning of the "search"; the captain said he was just checking his beat. Yet no resident dared try to stop the investigation; most just hid their outrage and indignation and forced a smile when the captain called them by their first names.

When I later pointed out to the officer the ill will he creates everywhere by his condescension and by invading the privacy of others, he looked astounded. He saw no reason why routine checks should bother the poor, why his attempts at pleasantries were offensive. No one had ever questioned his popularity before. No one had ever openly opposed him. Consequently, he thought he was doing just fine. How insensitive he was to the people, "his" people. How unprepared he was for ghetto service.

Emergency situations often turn into disasters because of the poor service offered the ghetto. Fire departments are often blamed for answering too late when Harlem or Watts or Hough calls. Firemen are often assailed for providing inadequate ambulance service. Hospitals are frequently too many miles away to make access easy. Watts, for example, is not only without any public hospital, but there is no such facility within ten miles of the area. The ride from Watts to the County General Hospital on public transportation takes approximately two hours.

In Chicago in 1960, there were about 500 beds available to blacks in private hospitals, while the city had a black population of 900,000. There was half a bed for every thousand blacks, four and a half beds for every thousand whites.[24]

Sanitation departments are notorious for the poor service they provide to areas which are most congested and are, therefore, in need of the greatest service. In Washington, D.C., a youth organization called Pride, Inc., was established to do the job the Sanitation Department left undone. For four weeks in the summer of 1967 1,080 youths were put to work full-time and

980 youths continued to work throughout the year to clean up the refuse and the rats the Sanitation Department neglected.

Ghetto areas don't get their share of recreational and cultural facilities either. There are no movies in Watts. In Harlem, there is no art gallery, no museum.

In 1964 parks and playgrounds constituted only 10 per cent of Harlem's acreage as compared with 16 per cent of all of New York City. What is worse, ". . . all the parks are esthetically and functionally inadequate . . ."[25] In Washington, a 1964 study revealed that the city's poorest 40 per cent had only two recreational areas less than the wealthiest 40 per cent, but they had a population which was almost 50 per cent more.[26]

NO WELCOME OUTSIDE

To make matters worse, blacks are not welcomed outside the ghetto, even in public places, and transportation departments often see to it that they don't venture forth. The Los Angeles transportation system that serviced Watts before the riots was perhaps the most flagrant example of a bus system which locked residents in. Actually, there was no one single bus system in Watts. There were four systems and one subsidiary; three of the systems were public, one and its subsidiary, private. The four different systems operated independently of each other, were uncoordinated, and free transfers between systems were not provided. One bus system, the Southern California Rapid Transit District, which provided the principal transportation in and out of the Watts area, did not provide free transfers to lines in outlying areas, nor to other lines within Watts. In addition, due to alleged increases in operating expenses, the systems have cut back services and increased fares over the years. The Southern California Rapid Transit District raised its basic fare five cents in July 1967. That was the second increase in fare in less than three months.

Space is usually available in the ghetto for that enterprise which is debilitating. Bars are everywhere. There are liquor stores by the hundreds. Striptease clubs lure the passersby. Fortune-tellers' doors are open, offering mystical charm, magical flights. The ghetto dwellers need these dens, for they offer an escape from all that is troublesome—indeed, from life itself. The white invader, too, needs these places for his occasional flights into oblivion and lust. Yet, the black man has to pay the price. It is his family which must daily be exposed to the sordidness lining the streets. It is his children who, on their way to and from school, see the prostitutes, the drunks and the addicts. The white man is home free, with all the pleasures and none of the pain.

And so the white Establishment agrees to close its eyes to all that is illegal as long as the twilight world can be enclosed behind walls, never to dawn in white backyards. As long as the evil doesn't threaten to spill over, officialdom looks aside.

The ghetto resident sees himself and his kind huddled together in an ever diminishing world. It is a world that is in a near state of siege, a world that suffers continuous bombardment by outside powers in the name of progress. The teacher, the policeman, the welfare worker, and every other official dispatched to "save" the ghetto cause increasing revulsion because ghetto residents eye the whole world of officialdom as one odious giant who, in stepping on them, is planning his next feat—rubbing them into the dirt with whatever power he can muster. They are convinced that the urban renewal official is out to rid them of their homes, the policeman is out to strip them of the little freedom they have left. No bureaucratic talk can lessen their suspicion, their fear, their distrust, their loathing.

A song once sung in ghetto churches expresses the depths of the ghetto dweller's misery:

> I am a pilgrim and a stranger,
> Traveling through this barren land,
> I have a home in yonder city,
> Over there, Lord, over there.

A similar sentiment was expressed to me by a man who sought help from the Urban League when his pay check couldn't cover his wife's sudden medical expenses and food to feed his children. He said, "When things get so bad I say to myself, they can't be this bad always, for someday I'm gonna die."

The ghetto resident knows that his life is doomed. His future will resemble the present just as the present is a copy of the past.

He can no longer hope. At best, he can endure. Only in death might he be able to find life. How reminiscent this is of "I am glad that trouble don't last always" and "By and by, I'm going to lay down my heavy load"—songs written and sung by slaves.

The Riot Commission concluded not long ago that "our nation is moving toward two societies, one black, one white—separate and unequal."[27] Are we not already there? Can there be any doubt that two worlds presently exist in America? They are separated, if not by actual walls, then by forces which achieve the same result. In one world, white men move with freedom; in the other, blacks are serving time.

You are still in jail, in the hole or out of the hole. You are still in jail in the street or behind bars. It is the same thing, a matter of existing. . . .

2

White Supremacy, Black Desperation

> The gods had condemned Sisyphus to ceaselessly rolling a rock to the top of a mountain whence the stone would fall back of its own weight. They had thought with some reason that there is no more dreadful punishment than futile and hopeless labor.[1]
>
> —Albert Camus

That white supremacy has damaged the lives and minds of millions of blacks in the South is an accepted fact in most quarters. That white supremacy has damaged the lives and minds of millions of blacks in the ghettos of the North is still challenged in those same quarters. Indeed, even many white liberals are reluctant to acknowledge the existence of white supremacy north of the Mason-Dixon line.

Yet, let him who doubts spend some time in any of America's black ghettos. Let him frequent the shops, the bars, the eating places and talk with the area residents. Let him enter the bank, the launderette, the corner market. Let him ask who owns each establishment, who does the hiring and the firing. Let him see who pockets the weekly rent, who doles out the welfare payments, who determines welfare eligibility.

It might take the objective observer all of three or four hours to realize that there exists somewhere an enchanted land where some white men live in opulence, their pockets padded with dollars earned for them by the sweat of the black man. It will not take him long to discern that black men are still virtually slaves to other Americans, that the men with the money are the men with the power, and that the black men with the marginal jobs are the men left with nothing.

CAUGHT UP IN A SYSTEM

It won't take him long to discern that through America's conscious activity—or perhaps because of its inactivity, its lethargy—a system has been allowed to develop which now generates its own power and which seems to run the lives of men. Indeed, it is a system so well developed that it catches everyone up in it. It shouts out the directions; men acquiesce for a complex of reasons and take the road down which they've been ordered or shoved.

By allowing themselves to become tools of the system, people perpetuate it and its inherent evils. White masses are just as guilty as white leadership because in tolerating injustices, in adjusting to society's inequities, by simply remaining silent, they compromise their own integrity and bid the evil endure.

The system catches the black man up in it, too, but perhaps for different reasons. The system shuts out most Negroes. But to increase its own respectability, it has allowed a few Negroes to move up—although never in. It hands out a few unimportant political front-desk jobs; it offers a few cash handouts. It gives a few black men a slight reward for allowing themselves to be used.

It may seem hard to understand how any black man could willingly cooperate with that system which cuts off his arms and legs and dares him to compete, a system which instructs black men to turn on their own kind, which teaches them that if they want to get out of the streets they've got to walk over the bodies strewn there, a system that teaches black men to act white. What motivates those who play ball with the enemy? Nothing short of utter desperation. That Negro who is desperate, hungry, and cold might not challenge his instructors for long. He has too little; he's been raped too often; he's forgotten how to fight back. He'll follow almost any door marked *exit* no matter where it leads.

There are others who are frustrated by the power of the system's controlling steel arm. They feel they are getting crushed, yet know they are powerless to stop the assault. They know they can't change the system—the best they can do is beat it. They, too, want glory, and a Cadillac brings it. What matter the compromises, as long as they go undetected?

The system legalizes immorality for some. It protects its whitest villains from the arm of the law. But for the black man who transgresses, it builds no shelter; indeed, it refuses even to open an umbrella. The black man's immoral acts are rarely sanctioned by the law; therefore, his misdeeds are more visible.

The rulers of this system, be they black or white, are, in large part, unconcerned about the plight of the nation's black serfs. As young ghetto blacks are growing up, society barrages them with testimony as to their worthlessness and its lack of concern. Children are still children when they learn all the negative connotations of *black* and see that most things good come to one who is white. Ossie Davis has eloquently pointed out that the word *blackness* has 120 definitions in *Roget's Thesaurus,* that 60 of these definitions have "distinctly unfavorable" connotations, and that none of the definitions even approaches the positive. *Whiteness,* on the other hand, with 134 synonyms, has 44 definitions with favorable connotations and only 10 definitions with mild negative implications.

> When you consider the fact that *thinking* itself is sub-vocal speech . . . one must use *words* in order to think at all—you will appreciate the enormous heritage of racial prejudgment that lies in wait for any child born into the English Language. Any teacher, good or bad, white or black, Jew or Gentile, who uses the English Language as a medium of communication is forced, willy-nilly, to teach the Negro child 60 ways to despise himself, and the white child 60 ways to aid and abet him in the crime.[2]

The self-fulfilling prophesy comes into play early. All human beings formulate their own feelings of adequacy and self-esteem on the impressions others have of them and transmit to them. The child who is daily reminded that he is not worthy of respect, the child who is continuously rejected and shown none of the common courtesies, will at an early age be victimized by parasitic self-doubts which will eventually eat away the core of his being—his dignity, his pride, his feelings of worth.

Kenneth and Mamie Clark discovered that three-year-old Negro children notably prefer a white doll to a brown one, feeling that the white doll is nicer, looks better, and has a better color.[3] Studies by Mary Ellen Goodman reveal that black nursery school children often fail to identify themselves as Negro and prefer to see themselves as white.[4] Four-year-old white children show "unmistakable signs of the onset of racial bigotry" while

> . . . Negro children not yet five can sense that they are marked, and grow uneasy. They can like enormously what they see across the color line, and find it hard to like what they see on their side. In this there is scant comfort or security, and in it are the dynamics for rending personality asunder.[5]

The human ego does not, and cannot, develop in a vacuum. It receives signals from the outside which it sifts through and studies. It sees itself through the lenses of others—it is free only to interpret the signals transmitted to it. This is what Harry S. Sullivan called "learning about self, from the mirror of other people." According to Arthur Combs, a psychologist and educator, a child develops feelings that he is ". . . liked, wanted, acceptable and able from *having been* liked, wanted, accepted and from *having been* successful."

> One learns that he is these things, not from being told so, but only through the experience of *being treated as though he were so*. . . . To produce a positive self, it is necessary to provide experiences that teach individuals they are positive people.[6]

Healthy growth is stunted, therefore, if the individual finds himself in an unwholesome climate, a climate formed by people who treat him as if he were inadequate and unwanted. Earl C. Kelley, a well-known educator, explains that when a person is forced to exist in an environment of this sort, he defensively withdraws into a "psychological shell," shutting off or distorting communication from the outside. "The self then is denied that which it feeds on. Without the stuff of growth, the self becomes less adequate, and the whole person loses its ability to do, to venture, to create."[7]

Hence, the child in school who is put into the slow track at a young age and is consequently treated as a non-learner builds defenses and will, in fact, become a non-learner. He will begin to see himself as his teachers and his classmates see him and lose whatever confidence he had; learning and growth slow down or stop prematurely.

For the black child, this early rejection in school is paralleled by other social rejections. Indeed, negative signs dart onto his consciousness at every turn: the rude white cop on the corner every morning; the indignities he hears his mother describe late at night, the indignities she faces in the white man's kitchen; his father's sometime job.

After hearing eighteen years of evidence, after being told so many times in so many different ways that he is of little value, insignificant, *de trop,* the black ghetto adolescent who doesn't feel inadequate and unworthy is the rarity—not because he has learned the right lesson, but because he has learned the only lesson he has ever been taught. He has internalized all he has seen and heard and is forever debilitated as a result.

Perhaps the hardest feeling to live with is that one's life really doesn't matter—that one's voice, one's feelings, one's ideas might just as well be forever choked down, unexpressed, for there is no one who will hear them, feel them or stop to evaluate them anyway.

Recently a group of ghetto poor from a section of northwest Washington banded together against granting a pool room license to someone who sought to build such an establishment in their neighborhood. Petition after petition was signed; almost every citizen in the neighborhood opposed opening the hall. Parents felt the pool room would be a bad influence on their children and feared it would quickly become a local hangout. The citizens' group went to see the police captain to present their thoughts and petitions. Despite the unanimity on the part of the people whose lives the pool hall would directly affect, the captain recommended that the license be granted. He reasoned that such a hall would be a good place to develop informers.

The ghetto dweller wakes up to the nightmare of invisibility and powerlessness early in the long night that is his life. He knows that most decisions concerning his life and that of his family are made without his knowledge, without his consent, and more often than not, against his better interest. When new freeways are proposed, it is his home which is on a collision course with the bulldozer. When new housing goes up on his property, his chances for reoccupancy are minimal at best. When the government passes social legislation, somewhere in the legislative web, in the writing of the regulations, or in the enforcement process, it gets limited so that he can't experience fully its intended benefits.

What is worse, unlike the African Negro or the West Indian who fought for independence, the black American has been fighting only for desegregation and integration, goals he can attain only if the ". . . white majority sanctions them as legitimate and desirable." The result is that

> Negroes do not determine the ends for which they struggle, nor the means. The most they can expect is an increasingly greater share in the joint determination of their future. The problem of maintaining dignity and some autonomy in such a situation is, for sensitive personalities, a continuous one . . .[8]

To be poor and to feel unworthy and powerless is bad enough; to be poor and feel unworthy and powerless in the midst of plenty is more than most could bear. Yet, the ghetto dweller need not look far to see the disparity between what he has and what others have. For whenever he looks in at the white world, be it through television ads or in the home of his employer, he sees luxury and the apparently carefree happiness of middle-class life—day jobs, playing space for children, refrigerators that are rarely empty, unfrayed clothing, solid shoes. All the luxuries. The comparison between what he observes and what he lives cannot but press hard on his consciousness. Some fight to grab the unreachable; a few Claude Browns touch a star. But most are overwhelmed by incomprehensible forces and either accept their plight, becoming cripplingly apathetic, or rebel by destructively acting out their vengeance against society, their brothers, or themselves.

TO STRUGGLE OR TO SUBMIT?

Life is either a continuous and demoralizing struggle or it is submission. There is no middle ground. Either one grabs and grabs and grabs, hands doomed to remain empty but thrashing about nonetheless in order to keep the circulation going—or one is grabbed, had, taken, controlled.

I met a young man last summer who was a grabber. He had a police record and couldn't find decent employment, so he began playing cards and cheating. He cheated, he said, because "no one wins by playing fair" and he had to win or his family wouldn't eat. For a time his hands were full, but he spent months hating himself and living in fear of detection. He might just as well have been destitute.

Those who are taken can be seen early each morning, from 5:30 a.m. on, on the streetcorners of every big city. In Washington, D.C., they wait on Fifth and K. They stand in the cold, in the heat, waiting for trucks to come by and pick up a helper for the day. Each time a truck or car approaches and slows down, the hungry men race into the street and plead for a day of work. The few who are lucky get meager wages for a long and tedious day. The unlucky ones get nothing. All get taken.

Most escape routes have been systematically and shrewdly cemented off. The youth who under other circumstances would challenge the system and find his way out never in the ghetto develops the motivation to do so. Indeed, in his world of truncated opportunity and underpreparedness, motivation has no place. It cannot be taught. Only a handful can generate it in isolation.

Of the few who actively seek escape from the ghetto, some do manage to find the cracks in the wall, but not before peeling off as much as is humanly possible of all that is ghetto, of all that is black. Otherwise the crack would be made visible and recemented before the escape was guaranteed.

Of those who remain, there are many who would never choose to venture forth, even if given the opportunity, because they feel their lives have meaning only within the context of the ghetto. Such individuals live with a false sense of worth, and they know it. Yet, they stay in the ghetto to protect this feeling of significance, however unreal and distorted, because it is all that they have left. Their security comes from a common denominator of insufficiency. Once they leave their contrived world, values change. Each rightly fears that an encounter with the white man's system would force him to come face to face with himself and his failures. He understandably prefers the security of the ghetto.

According to Samuel D. Proctor, this fear of the ghetto dweller is a direct result of the social rejection that is his daily fare. "Fear is the automatic response that the ego requires when it is threatened, when it is vetoed, thwarted, or suppressed with no escape." Dr. Proctor goes on to point out that while such a person may be wearing a ". . . mask of bravery and Spartan-like courage . . . he is really very frightened."

He is afraid of big words, afraid of polite company, afraid of large, clean rooms, afraid of printed tests, afraid of the presence of successful people, afraid of those in authority, and afraid of being left alone to examine his life. Observe that he stays in the street and among those people who demand nothing of him but who take him as he is.[9]

Perhaps the plight of this large group of individuals is the greatest tragedy of all. White America forces them to create fantasies and gives them a place to live where their delusions need never be challenged, where suffering and hardship are commonplace and where they can measure themselves against others in direr straights and appear heroic in juxtaposition. It is the white power wielders who sentence black men to serve life in this place, for they are the ones who have made escape suicidal. Escape means a return to reality and failure. Better to live on and harbor false dreams and unchallenged illusions.

A strange kind of freedom, this. A man is free to hover in the gutter of the ghetto with others whose conditions parallel his own. A man is free to dream of power, of pride, of accomplishment, of wealth, but free never to taste of them. This is freedom at its most macabre. It is the freedom of the chained. As Ralph Ellison put it: "But what do *I* really want, I've asked myself. Certainly not the freedom of a Rinehart or the power of a Jack, nor simply the freedom not to run. No, but the next step I couldn't make, so I've remained in the hole."[10]

Yet, the history books of this country are replete with tales of America's successes in guaranteeing freedom to all. In *Forever Free,* Dorothy Sterling describes the Emancipation Proclamation in these terms:

For almost two hundred and fifty years slaves on the North American continent had struggled to break their chains. At last the world's first democracy had caught up with its promise of liberty and equality for all.[11]

From *History of Our United States:*

America has thrived and prospered because most of her people have worked hard to develop and to protect a special kind of mental climate—a climate in which freedom can flourish.[12]

From *American Government:*

From the time of the founding of our nation to the present, we have preserved and extended freedom. And we are determined to go on doing so.[13]

And, from *The Citizen and His Government:*

The thrill of America and American history may be condensed into one word—Freedom.

Freedom! It is much more than just a word. It means that all have equal rights, many of which are not written in laws. A free person has the right to "count for something," to take part in the affairs of the community and the nation, to search for a better job, to raise his standard of living. . . . and, because we live in a nation founded on the principle of equality for all, every American can expect his government to guarantee freedom of opportunity in securing those rights.[14]

Many of the country's leaders sing loud their own praises for giving so much to so many, for seeing to it that all chains are unlocked. Yet, the progress they cite and the optimism they muster are not seen or shared by the Negro masses who see a different America.

A black antipoverty worker upon graduation from high school in Ohio was given a present, a trip to New York. As his airplane was circling the city, he beckoned to the stewardess and with a frown asked what that green statue with the books and torch was.

The stewardess looked surprised but dutifully answered, "Why, can't you tell, that's the Statue of Liberty."

"But," he replied, "there's something wrong with it. Don't you think she ought to be turned around or put on a turntable so that some of us Americans might be able to see that this is the land of the free?"

When he began his sightseeing, his first stop was the Statue of Liberty. He went up close so he could read the inscription:

> . . . Give me your tired, your poor,
> Your huddled masses yearning to be free,
> The wretched refuse of your teeming shore.
> Send these, the homeless, tempest tossed, to me. . . .

The recent high school graduate stopped, stretched out his arms, smiled, and said, "Baby, here we are!"

Haven't most politicians really forgotten the "huddled masses" as they allow themselves to get caught up in their own fancy rhetoric? When all the political hoopla dies down, when the air is let out of the inflated verbiage, what is left? Just what has America done to guarantee freedom, to provide equality of opportunity, to equalize the life chances of the poor, the black?

FREED ONLY TO BE RE-ENSLAVED

During the slavery period, there was no freedom, no opportunity at all. When the Civil War ended and the slaves were freed, the country acted as though it had purged itself of all guilt. That the whites had loosened black chains was a selfless and benevolent act. And there began and ended their responsibility. Hence, the black man was left free to deal with starvation, poverty, and want, for there was little, if any, opportunity afforded him. Where could he take his new-found freedom? What could he do with it? He had been torn from his family, was virtually uneducated, and, for the most part, untrained for all but the most menial of tasks. The door was blocked before he ever had a chance to walk through. His black skin condemned him to remain on the outside looking in, in a land where nothing on the periphery mattered. Could the whites really have believed that they had liberated the blacks?

Southern whites worked fast to re-enslave the black man. By 1867, eight southern states had passed Black Codes. In South Carolina these codes stated that freedmen could not enter any occupation ". . . except that of a farmer or servant, unless they secured a special license and paid an annual tax." In Louisiana, farm or plantation workers had to sign a contract promising to fulfill its terms or forfeit all wages. In Florida, freedmen who didn't fulfill contract provisions or who were "impudent" to their employer were subject to punishment for vagrancy.[15]

The era of separate but equal was ushered in by the Supreme Court decision of 1896 which declared constitutional a Louisiana law stating that "all railway companies carrying passengers in their coaches in this state shall provide equal but separate accommodations for the white and colored races."[16] That the country reversed the adjectives *equal* and *separate* and thereby changed the emphasis if not the meaning of the decision is significant. Indeed, in the wake of the Court action, the nation expunged *equal* from its consciousness and launched a campaign to achieve separation—schools, buses, toilet facilities, restaurants, water fountains, movie houses, as well as railroad cars as far north as Washington, D.C., Maryland, Pennsylvania, and Missouri became either white or black. And the whites got the best that there was; the Negroes got what happened to be left.

That separate accommodations for whites and blacks might be incompatible with the Fourteenth Amendment's promise of the "equal protection of the laws" was strongly denied by Henry B. Brown who wrote the majority opinion for the Supreme Court in Plessy v. Ferguson:

> . . . the amendment . . . could not have been intended to abolish distinctions based upon color, or to enforce social, as distinguished from political, equality, or a commingling of the two races upon terms unsatisfactory to either. . . .
>
> Legislation is powerless to eradicate racial instincts or to abolish distinctions based upon physical differences, and the attempt to do so can only result in accentuating the difficulties of the present situation. . . . If one race be inferior to the other socially, the Constitution of the United States cannot put them on the same plane.[17]

"Separate but equal" all but established a caste system in the United States, for it offered first class citizenship to those born white, and relegated to a lowly status those born black. And the concept of different types of citizenship for different Americans won strong approval from all quarters. Rayford Logan points out that

At the beginning of the twentieth century, what is now called second-class citizenship for Negroes was accepted by presidents, the Supreme Court, Congress, organized labor, the General Federation of Women's Clubs—indeed by the vast majority of Americans, North and South. . . .[18]

Two worlds had been reborn, if indeed either had ever stopped breathing. The black world was given half its birthright—the rest the white master swiped.

In the 1950's, the country began to awaken anew to its internal contradictions, to its hypocrisy, to the disparity between its stated beliefs and its actions. The Brown decision clearly repudiated the separate but equal doctrine by stating that ". . . in the field of public education the doctrine of 'separate but equal' has no place. Separate educational facilities are inherently unequal."[19] Yet, as though in fear of its own strength, the Court in the following year issued a decree in which it let everyone off the hook—everyone, that is, but the Negro who again got pierced, this time with unexpected jabs.

In ruling that lower courts must supervise the disengagement of segregated school systems with "all deliberate speed," it allowed each locality to define "deliberate" and "speed" for itself. Hence, the Court undercut its own power, guaranteeing further victories for the white supremacists.

In the 1960's, the civil rights battle, with new-found momentum and support, raged its way into Congressional chambers, onto the Senate and House floors. Some good legislation was passed, some adequate enforcement power was granted administrative agencies. Yet, to date, the equality promised by the Civil Rights Acts has been withheld from the black man.

Over the years, black men got the hint. Some gave up trust and hope before others and decided early that there would be no equal protection for the black man unless it was fought for and demanded of the executive, the legislative and the judicial branches of the government. If blacks wanted basic rights, they would have to organize and press hard for them. And so, early in the 1900's the National Association for the Advancement of Colored People was founded and began to work within the framework of government and established institutions to close the racial gap. The organization's skillful lawyers began a long tradition of judicial battles and won many courtroom victories. Later the NAACP established a Washington bureau lobby and thus carried its work into the halls of Congress, clubbing away at injustices, attempting to knock down old prejudices, rooting out entrenched discrimination.

The Urban League was born in 1910 when Negroes in Northern cities decided that they were experiencing problems similar to those they had faced down South. The only difference was that in the haven of the liberal, free North, the controls were not written into law. But they were there and everybody knew them and operated accordingly. The Urban League decided to use the conference table to end discrimination in the big city.

But despite the efforts of the organized civil rights groups, progress was slow and painstaking. The creaking machinery of the courts seemed to defy its challengers to persevere. Briefs gathered dust and freedom was held in abeyance while judges deliberated on legal technicalities. Congress got educated somewhat by the lobbying efforts that were made in hushed phrases behind closed doors, but in the final analysis most decisions were made to please the constituency, one's own conscience be damned. The conference table approach was fraught with other problems, not the least of which was that the black man had little bargaining power and could fight only from a position of weakness. The only trump in his pocket was often the rightness of his cause, and that, apparently, counted for little.

During the 1950's and early 60's when the mood of white America began to change, when it evidenced more understanding and more concern that ever before, the ghetto showed signs of increasing restlessness. The black man felt he was no closer to his goal, and it was apparent to anyone interested in reading the signs that poor blacks were fed up. James Baldwin quotes an anonymous Negro who expressed the wrath, the disaffection, the grieved impatience of the ghetto: "At the rate things are going here, all of Africa will be free before we can get a lousy cup of coffee."[20]

To the ghetto black, the big words of the Brown Court decision were but a fancy, polished veneer which glossed over his immediate needs. The gains, the paper progress, that were heralded as the beginning of a new era never even aroused him.

His feelings and his impatience were expressed by the freedom rides, the sit-ins, the marches which followed. Court decisions, legislative efforts, arbitration—all had failed. No more would the black man wait in silence for miracles. The revolution had begun. The tone of the movement changed. Bayard Rustin wrote, "The war cry is 'unconditional surrender—end all Jim Crow now.' Not next week, not tomorrow—but now."[21]

From behind bars, Martin Luther King wrote:

I guess it is easy for those who have never felt the stinging darts of segregation to say wait. But when you have seen vicious mobs lynch your mothers and fathers at will and drown your sisters and brothers at whim; when you have seen hate-filled policemen curse, kick, brutalize, and even kill your black brothers and sisters with impunity . . . when your first name becomes "nigger" and your middle name becomes "boy" . . . then you will understand why we find it difficult to wait. There comes a time when the cup of endurance runs over.[22]

John Killens' anger burst forth from the page:

My fight is not to be a white man in a black skin, but to inject some black blood, some black intelligence into the pallid mainstream of American life, culturally, socially, psychologically, philosophically.

. . . now, in the middle of the 20th century, I, the Negro, am refusing to be your "nigrah" any longer. Even some of us "favored," "talented," "unusual" ones are refusing to be your educated, sophisticated, split-level "nigrahs" any longer. We refuse to look at ourselves through the eyes of white America.[23]

The white man's reaction to a new, invigorated civil rights movement could have been predicted. He protested the change in tactics and the new radicalism while, at the same time, he sought to scrape off a few more crumbs to throw to the hungry. He came up with the Civil Rights Acts of 1964 and 1965. Both acts, if enforced, could have made a difference, but each was sabotaged by spineless, scared administrators whose ears were tuned to Pennsylvania Avenue and Capitol Hill, not the American ghettos. And so, the man in the ghetto was again victimized.

THE CHARISMA OF BLACK POWER

Against this backdrop, it should surprise no one in this country that the cries of black power rang an immediate responsive chord in 1966 in the ghetto. For black power advocates began to do what everyone else had failed to do—they recognized the meekest, the most oppressed, and worked to reach them. No ivory tower message, theirs. Theirs was the message of the street told in a language that was comprehensible because it was told by people of the street.

Black power appears to be an opportunity to many. It helps men piece together shattered self-images. It helps them to start to live. It restores racial pride. An eighteen-year-old was able to write:

> I am Black,
> Black in mind that is.
> For once I was white,
> I was a Tom.
>
> I was lost,
> But now I'm found,
> Lost in white
> Found to Black.
>
> Now I am Free.
> Free from the boundaries of the white man.
> Free to walk Black, talk Black,
> Think Black and be Black.
>
> I am Black.
> I am proud.
> For Black is beauty.
> And Black is inferior to no one and nothing.[24]

It is true that there are many ghetto blacks who are ambivalent toward and confused by the whole black power movement. They are not sure if it is a form of therapy or a more damaging sickness. They don't know whether it will insulate or isolate, whether it will really strengthen their pride or simply provide one more mechanism to ward off society's blows through a new kind of self-deception. They wonder whether it is simply a device without a program, a device which will cause them to deceive themselves into believing they are something they really aren't, that they can achieve something that is still out of reach for blacks in America.

But beneath all the doubts, most feel proud of the ghetto-inspired, ghetto-grown movement. Its charisma is appealing. Its leaders defy the very power structures which keep the black man in bondage.

Most white Americans have convinced themselves that the Rap Browns of the country cause the Cambridges; that the Cambridges of the country don't cause the Rap Browns. They deceive themselves, for despite the appeal of the language and the style of the black power movement, despite the power of its leaders, it is not these elements which instill in ghetto dwellers the animosity they feel toward the white man. It is not these elements which stir and incite the ghetto to act out its hostility. Rather, it is the despair and desperation which result from the powerlessness, the hopelessness and the Sisyphus-like struggles that are the ghetto's mainstay which sow the seeds of riot and rebellion. People who have nothing and who think they are nothing have nothing to lose by seeking recognition, however violently. And it sometimes just feels good to dole out violence when one has been only its victim.

What stirs ghetto blacks to violence is years of white misdeeds compounded by more years of more misdeeds. It is years of white supremacy which rankle, not a few anguished but eloquent black cries.

There was a time when the hatred of the ghetto, the hatred of the Negro, was selective. The white persons who meted out the injustices were the persons the black man loathed. Today, the black man's hatred has generalized to all that is white. He no longer stops to single out the whites who are atypical, the whites who don't have a stake in maintaining America's racist attitudes and practices. Even the white liberal fighting discrimination is often regarded unkindly. The black man is no longer selective in his hatred, but then, the white man was never selective in his discrimination.

I once spoke with a Negro doctor who had been born in Georgia, who had left the South to attend college, medical school, and to establish a practice, and who had decided to return to visit his home state a few years back. As he neared his destination, his daughter became ill and he stopped at a gas station so that she might use the rest room. She was forthwith advised that no such facilities were available to "nigrahs," that the rest room she saw was for the exclusive use of whites. That her father didn't force the attendant to allow her to use the facility troubled the child. That he could not be a man before his own children almost destroyed the prominent physician. His hatred of whites surfaced—he had no desire to try and intellectualize about the white man's racial hang-ups any longer.

There is something almost perverse about that society which allows the white gas attendant to set the rules. Something perverse about a society which allows such individuals to terrorize and emasculate others. Something perverse about a society which guarantees to every black man numerous encounters with the white gas station attendant.

3

Is the Black Ghetto Unique?

> . . . the Negro of today is an internal migrant who will face racism wherever he goes, who cannot leave his oppression behind as if it were a czar or a potato famine.[1]
>
> —MICHAEL HARRINGTON

There are many myths which are gaining increasing acceptance in minority group circles as the Negro in America presses harder for recognition and power. Such myths are often nothing but rationalizations spun to enclose their espousers in a web of deceit; intensified and thickened to keep out light, to keep the image-makers from seeing their own pernicious prejudices; spun and respun, time and again, as though repetition could somehow give meaning to the activity, make it more convincing, more authentic.

A TYRANNY OF BODY AND SOUL

The first such myth is of the "we-were-slaves-too-and-we-overcame" variety. The creators of this myth argue that Negroes, like some other minorities, were enslaved and that is shameful. But, the would-be historians hasten to add, slavery has ended for the black man the same way it has ended for the Jew, the Slav, the European peasant. It's time to get on with living. There's no need for the Negro citizen to dwell in the ignominy of his past, and there is no need to compensate him in the present for events long since buried, for in a democracy he is as free as the next man to enter into the mainstream of life.

The underlying assumptions in this argument are that the Negro labored under a system of slavery comparable to systems which oppressed other groups, that one system of slavery parallels all others, and that, therefore, the results of bondage are the same on all who are or were enslaved. Such assumptions are unfounded and totally distort historical truths.

The slavery known in most parts of the world from ancient times on was maintained by a system of chains and the threat or the reality of death. In Cuba, slaves worked the sugar plantations, subject to long hours, exceedingly cruel overseers, and harsh work that accounted for high mortality rates. Slave hunters called *rancheadores* solved the problem of the runaway, using methods that at one time did not stop short of castration. In Rome, slaves worked half naked in mines, goaded on by the brutal lash of the commanding soldier. In Brazil's period of slavery, a vast array of tortuous instruments was used to punish the cantankerous slave—the *tronco,* an instrument of wood or iron, was placed upon the slave's ankles; the *limbambo* was used to grip a wayward slave at the neck; the *algemas* and *anjinhos* were used to hold the slave's hands and crush his thumbs. Often the more brutal master tied a disobedient Negro slave face down on the ground and beat him with a whip of rawhide on each of nine to thirteen consecutive nights.

Such ruling masters retained their power by inflicting upon their slaves innumerable physical controls and tortures. Yet, in most cases, the slave was left with some dignity and some self-respect. In Cuba, the slave had legal rights such as marriage, parenthood and fraternization. The law considered him to be a ". . . human being, a legal personality possessing . . . innumerable rights as well as obligations."[2] The Romans viewed slavery as a normal condition of man. It was an affliction that befell an individual because that individual was unfortunate and unlucky, not because of his undesirability or his subhuman nature. In Brazil, a paternalistic Church considered the slave a human being with an immortal soul. The mistreated slave could appeal to Church authorities for ". . . redress of his wrongs, and in practice this was not an empty provision of the legal code of the colony."[3] In addition, there was respect for the sanctity and the integrity of the slave family.

But many American slaveholders, nineteenth-century style, set their own precedents and played out their tyranny on body and soul alike. Their slaves were deemed subhuman creatures and, in most cases, were accorded no rights. Slaveholders attempted not only to keep their black men from freedom, but also to kill in them the desire to obtain freedom. The white American slaveholder wanted to control and mold the minds of his "possessions"; physical sacrifice was not enough. Consequently, he encouraged—demanded—ignorance. He believed, and perhaps rightly, that the Southern way of life would be in jeopardy were the slaves to become educated. His fears were incorporated into the slave codes which prohibited teaching or allowing Negro slaves to read and write. As Kenneth Stampp described it:

> No person, not even the master, was to teach a slave to read or write, employ him in setting type in a printing office, or give him books or pamphlets. A religious publication asked rhetorically: "Is there any great moral reason why we should incur the tremendous risk of having our wives slaughtered in consequence of our slaves being taught to read incendiary publications?" They did not need to read the Bible to find salvation: "Millions of those now in heaven never owned a bible."[4]

Stanley Elkins goes even further in describing the types of controls that were placed on a slave's mind by presenting a vivid and convincing comparison between the Southern slave plantation and the German concentration camps. He points out that both the Negro slave and the camp inmate were made to rely totally on the ruling authorities, to the extent that both were ". . . reduced to complete and childish dependence upon their masters. . . ." and became incapable of thinking and doing for themselves. What is worse,

> In a system as tightly closed as the plantation or the concentration camp, the slave's or prisoner's position of absolute dependency virtually compels him to see the authority-figure as somehow really "good." Indeed, all the evil in his life may flow from this man—but then so also must everything of any value. Here is the seat of the only "Good" he knows, and to maintain his psychic balance he must persuade himself that the good is in some way dominant.[5]

The only way to justify the existence of slavery in a democracy is by making the slave dependent, incapable of existing by himself in freedom. Since slaveholders did have to justify the apparent contradiction between the belief in freedom and the practice of slavery, they purposefully chose to establish a system which made the black man totally reliant. In the process, they gained absolute power—and a rationale.

It is irrelevant for this argument whether the slaveholders had Dr. Elkin's intellectual abilities and could truly penetrate the full meaning of what they were doing to those they held in bondage. What is significant is that in a few months the Nazis were able to transform completely successful, dignified and mature adults into unthinking, sychophantic, twittering children. It didn't take long at all to utterly alter the personalities and minds of people whose behavior patterns had developed for over fifty years. Think what they could have accomplished had they ruled one hundred years! Think what they could have accomplished with the minds of infants and children!

The existence of slavery itself does not explain why American Negroes remain buried in the ruins of an ignoble past, invisible men years after their liberation. Jews look to their period of enslavement with great pride. They seek never to hide or forget. Slavic people evidence no shame of their fettered pasts and seek not to tread softly over them. Such groups, however, have backgrounds almost antithetical to those of the black man. They were not killed off spiritually. Their families were not pulled asunder. They were not stripped of their names, forced to forget a rich heritage and a language all their own. Most important, defeat was not part of their final victory.

On the other hand, the black man's final humiliation is that he didn't even assist in tearing off his own chains. Rather, he was but a pawn in a power struggle, ". . . freed by others, as a by-product of a political dispute between two groups of whites."[6] He was freed not because freedom was deemed his birthright, but because one of the country's greatest leaders, President Lincoln, felt that the abolition of slavery would aid the North in winning the war and would eventually serve to strengthen the Union. As he himself wrote:

My paramount object in this struggle is to save the Union. . . . If I could save the Union without freeing any slave I would do it, and if I could save it by freeing all the slaves I would do it; and if I could save it by freeing some and leaving others alone, I would also do that. What I do about slavery and the colored race, I do because I believe it helps to save this Union. . . .[7]

So freedom was granted by the enemy, the best of whom was not even willing to admit that the white man had transgressed, that slavery was a grave moral injustice, that the black man mattered. Victory was swarthed in shame.

Given this peculiar brand of slavery which thwarted action and deadened thought, it should come as no surprise that in the entire period of Southern slavery there were but three major slave revolts. It should also be understood that this—probably the most egregious brand of slavery the world has ever known—had to produce a slave who differed significantly from the slave who suffered only bodily injustices. The Southern slave was bound to become more debilitated and less capable of dealing with freedom when it was eventually tasted. To equate the descendants of the Negro slaves with other slaves is to equate unequal quantities.

The final fallacy in the "we-were-slaves-too-forget-the-past" argument is that today cannot be separated from yesterday for the Negro American. Yesterday is part of a continuum and, therefore, is part of today's problem. What is happening today is precisely because of yesterday; the nature of today's problems is shaped by yesterday's occurrences. The vestiges of slavery are very much alive in the twentieth-century black ghettos as the preceding chapter demonstrated. If the past is to be buried, it must first die. And white America is working hard to keep it breathing.

BLACK IS DIFFERENT

The second myth is the oft-stated "You-are-no-different-than-we" with the implied corollary "so you should be able to assimilate as we did." Yet, let the utterers of this easy truism be faced with a proposal to integrate their schools, their neighborhoods, and their families, and an emotional enunciation of these nonexistent differences will assuredly be forthcoming.

There *is* a difference between the Negro migrant to the city and the Scotch, Irish, Polish and all other migrants who came to

America in the 1800's. The Negro is black. And blackness is adjudged evil in America. It is not wanted outside the ghetto; it is barely tolerated in the ghetto.

A few years back, I went to Canton, Ohio, on a business trip. Preoccupied with thoughts concerning my mission there, I inadvertently forgot to give the taxi driver my destination. And the driver didn't seek to ascertain it until we had reached the Negro section of town!

I later moved to Canton to become Executive Director of the Urban League there and discovered that the only way I could acquire decent housing was to build it or have it built myself. The patterns of segregated housing were so entrenched that all Negroes lived in the southwest sector of the city—even the doctors; conditions were deplorable.

When blacks seek admission into white society, many whites never stop to look beyond skin color, beyond the shallow, shabby stereotypes. Ralph Bunche, replete with Ph.D., Phi Beta Kappa key, and world renown, could not move into Cicero, Illinois, but Al Capone could and did! West Indian immigrants in the early 1900's, with their high educational achievements and superior business acumen, were not able to find housing outside the black ghettos.

In many Ohio communities prior to World War II there were no patterns of residential segregation because there were not many Negroes. As industry started to recruit during the war, Negroes arrived by the bus and train load. Residential segregation was instituted almost immediately.

The new residents were not arriving to go on welfare; they weren't coming as paupers with outstretched hands. They had been recruited by white industries and were going to earn good wages, so the prejudice and the resistance to them were not a function of economic status. White resistance to blacks had nothing whatever to do with personality or character either, for there wasn't time for such qualities to be assessed. The Negroes were siphoned off because of their color.

Blackness is always highly visible, but it is particularly visible in that society which distrusts it. The European immigrant, to be sure, was also visible with his accent, his native customs, his strange mode of dress, his long, un-American name, but each of these stigmas could be eradicated by an act of will. In a generation or two, accents could become so slight as to pass unnoticed, old customs could be replaced by new ones or could be practiced in the privacy of the home, clothing could be purchased as soon as there was money to spare, and those who were truly desirous of "melting in" could change their family names by filing a few papers in City Hall. At such a point assimilation would be guaranteed, for it is hard for society to discriminate against its minority group members when it isn't sure who they are. Thus, the European immigrant, in time, could penetrate the social barriers, unnoticed if he so desired. For many, the sacrifice was worthwhile.

The Negro, like the immigrant, has been cut off from all that was his former land. For centuries he has had no African name. He has no African religion. He practices no African customs. What is more, the overwhelming majority of American Negroes know of no relative born anyplace other than America. Yet the Negro still does not have the same choices open to him that were, and are, open to other newcomers to the city, for he wears an ineradicable badge of difference—his skin—and it is this badge which is responsible for his being "blackballed" out of the mainstream of American life. Nothing else matters, neither degrees, skills, nor wealth.

America has come to foster two antithetical ideologies, both with pride. The first, referred to above, is the melting pot idea. In this democratic country which houses so many different kinds of people from so many different countries and cultures, the final glory will come in the melting together of all the dissimilar elements to produce one great, united nation. As people become fused together, traces of differences will disappear, making possible a truer form of brotherhood.

At the other end of the pole, yet seen by many to be somehow consistent with the melting pot theory, is the belief in individual differences. America will be greatest if it agrees to allow its diverse populations to exhibit whatever differences they have, chastising and penalizing none for its disinclination to conform. By allowing each individual and each group this type of meaningful freedom, creativity will not be squelched and true democracy can be practiced.

According to Charles Silberman, the melting pot ideal has failed:

> . . . the crucial thing about the melting pot was that it did not happen: American politics and American social life are still dominated by the existence of sharply-defined ethnic groups. To be sure, these groups have been transformed by several generations of life in America; the immigrants of three or four or five generations ago would be unable to recognize the Italian-Americans, the Irish-Americans, the Jewish-Americans of the 1960s; the latter groups, in turn, would disavow kinship with their ancestors. And yet the ethnic groups are not just a political anachronism; they are a reality. The WASPs (White Anglo-Saxon Protestants), the Irish-Americans, the Italian-Americans, the Jewish-Americans do differ from each other in essential ways. They vote differently, raise their children differently, have different ideas about sex, education, religion, death, etc. . . . in truth there is no "white American"; there are only white Americans.[8]

Perhaps this is as it should be. The melting pot theory is objectionable because its underlying expectation is that an individual will give up his differences, his essence if you will, for a larger good and in order to gain full acceptance. For the black man this means milking his color to gain entrée into white neighborhoods and schools. It means talking white, acting white, and thinking white, whatever that means, to gain passage. Regardless of Silberman's contention, it is not so clear that the melting pot ideal is not still exerting a real force on the Negro in America, for talking white, acting white and thinking white are exactly what is being asked of him. Every black man knows that he must pass for white before he will gain full acceptance by his own society.

It is clear that the acceptance of individual differences is the more noble of the two goals, yet one is hard put to find examples of this ideal in practice as it pertains to the Negro-American. Indeed, America rejects those whose *only* difference is skin color. The country practices discrimination based upon race while enunciating high-sounding egalitarian ideals. But the ideals fall flat when juxtaposed against realities: In 1967, the unemployment rate for nonwhites was twice as high as it was for whites, the black family's income was 58 per cent of the white's income, a black man remained about three times as likely to hold a job as a laborer or as a service worker than a white man, black students tested at levels far below those of their white counterparts,[9] and in 1966, it was estimated that black colleges spent two-thirds of what white schools spent on the education of their students.[10]

Negroes are, furthermore, considered Negroes first. We have a national habit of talking about black Americans and white Americans, rather than Americans. When Thurgood Marshall was appointed to the Supreme Court, the headlines splashed "First Negro Supreme Court Justice." When Major Robert H. Lawrence, Jr., died in a crash, the headlines read "Negro Astronaut." As Frank Tannebaum put it:

> It is not enough to say, as we often do, that there are so many Negro doctors, lawyers, politicians, businessmen, and scholars. It is requisite that there should not be Negro doctors, Negro lawyers, or Negro scholars. Their professional standing must overshadow their racial origin. It is only when we can say he is a great actor, a great scholar, a great lawyer, a great citizen that the step has been taken which endows the Negro with the moral worth as a man which obliterates the invidious distinction and sweeps away the condescending fawning of the better-than-thou attitude.[11]

The blackness of the ghetto and the chains which the black man has ben unable to cut loose from slavery days are the components which make the black ghettos. It has already been shown that in a land where color prejudice exists, the blacks who can't lose their color have little hope of gaining entry into society at large. Their fate is then to remain in the ghetto. The European immigrants did not face this problem. They could mingle and they have mingled in large numbers, for their assimilation lotions are easier to apply—and bring the promised results!

COMPARISON WITH OTHER GROUPS IS NOT VALID

By way of introducing the third myth, an excerpt from a noted work written in 1951:

> Existing on the tenuous income supported by unskilled labor, they could not buy homes, nor could they lay out much in payment of rent. . . . The result was they got as little as possible.

. . . the unprepared cities had not ready the housing. . . . The newcomers were driven to accept hand-me-downs, vacated places . . .

. . . their first homes [were] in quarters the old occupants no longer desire. . . . To spend money on the repair or upkeep of houses in such areas is only wasteful; they will soon be torn down to make way for commercial buildings. The simplest, most profitable use is to divide the old mansions into tiny lodgings. . . .

. . . middle-class homes thus become laborers'—only not one to a family, but shared among many. What's more, behind the original structures are grassy yards where children once had run about at play. There is no room for games now. Sheds and shanties hurriedly thrown up, provide living space. . . . ingenuity has uncovered still other resources: fifteen hundred cellars also do service as homes.

. . . As the population continued to grow, and the demand with it, perspicacious owners of real estate saw profit in the demolition of the old houses and the construction, between narrow alleys, of compact barracks that made complete use of every inch of earth.

. . . everything is in poor repair, the rain comes through the ceilings, the wind blows dirt through the cracks in the wall. . . .

The very simplest tasks become complex and disorganizing. . . . The filthy streets are seldom cleaned; the municipality is not particularly solicitous of these, the poorest quarters of the city. . . . The inaccessible alleys and rear yards are never touched and, to be sure, are redolent of the fact. In the hot summer months the stench of rotting things will mark these places and the stained snow of winter will not conceal what lies beneath. . . .

Disorganization affects particularly the life of the home. . . . many traditional activities wither and disappear. Not here will the friends be welcome . . . children taught, and the family unite to share in the warmth of its security. Emptied of the meaning of these occurrences and often crowded with strange lodgers, home is just the feeding and sleeping place. All else moves to the outside.

. . . All relationships become less binding, all behavior more dependent on individual whim. The result was a marked personal decline and a noticeable wavering of standards.[12]

The author is Oscar Handlin, the book *The Uprooted,* and the excerpts a description of the life of the immigrants who came to

America in the middle 1800's. That the description could be, or was, mistaken for a statement on today's black ghettos is likely. The parallels are shockingly real—witness the physical decay, emotional instability, lack of privacy, total chaos.

And it is precisely these similarities which encourage the creation of the third myth which could well be entitled the "we-made-it-by-ourselves" syndrome. Its perpetrators claim that they came to America, if not enslaved then poverty-stricken, homeless, with no knowledge of the land, its customs and its language. Even if not encouraged, these self-made men will go on at great length to describe, in earthy fashion, life as they knew it in the Italian, the Irish, and the Polish ghettos. Jobs were scarce, times were tough. The foreigner was taken advantage of because he was desperate, because he couldn't understand what his oppressors were saying and what they were doing. Tables were empty and sickness was commonplace. Yet, somehow, through an ill-defined combination of drive and wits, they managed to make it—and without any help. Somehow, they began the slow ascent which their children, educated in American schools and speaking the English language, continue. In two or three generations they had tasted success, prosperity, comfort.

It is difficult to censure these pride-filled immigrants for distorting the truth, because it is fact that they began their lives in America in abject penury. Oscar Handlin is not the only historian who has put their struggles into words that Americans might see what many wished to hide from our national consciousness.

It is possible to censure these hearty pioneers only when they compare their plight with that of the Negro and conclude with the assumption that the Negro should be able to accomplish the same feats they accomplished with no additional difficulties, only when they reason that all groups relegated to the cellars of society have the same handicaps.

In his enthusiasm many a self-made immigrant overlooks the fact that the Negro is black. Enough has been said on that point. He also forgets that the job market today differs considerably from what it was in the 1800's when he came from Europe. The immigrant did not need any skills in order to qualify for a job, ". . . for first- and second-generation machines of the industrial revolution were creating a multitude of unskilled and semi-skilled jobs."[13] Most of the time before the Civil War, there were not enough people to meet the heavy labor requirements in the city and on the farm. Factories needed more and more hands—between the Civil War and World War I, manufacturing productivity multiplied twelvefold. As Conot put it, "The immigrant was exploited, but he was seldom frozen out of a job."[14]

On the other hand, there is little room in the employment market today for the man who is untrained and unskilled. Automation and new management techniques have simultaneously given birth to sundry new types of white-collar jobs while they have killed off hundreds of thousands of blue-collar opportunities. White-color jobs account for 97 per cent of the net increase in employment between 1947 and 1963.[15] In 1900, white-collar workers represented only about 16 per cent of the total labor force;[16] today white-collar workers represent 47 per cent of the force.[17] The man with no schooling, the man with inferior schooling, be he white or black, loses out time and again to his educational superior.

What is more, as Max Ways has shown, the immigrant who came to the city in the nineteenth century found a strong government—"unofficial and corrupt," but strong. It was a government that was willing to care for the immigrant, his family, his problems. "Such help as the clubhouse could give was inexpert and performed at a heavy, though hidden, social cost by such devices as loading city and traction company payrolls with incompetent workers." But the immigrant knew that City Hall ". . . was on his side, that it was aware of him in his whole humanity . . ."

The twentieth-century Negro migrant found a "castrated" City Hall, a City Hall that ". . . did not really control the autonomous departments into which urban services had become clotted." He found ". . . a system that . . . [had] lost its unity, its heart, that will not reach out with warmth toward where he is, a system where municipal institutions are no longer stirred by the great missionary and merchandising cry: 'Bring them in!' "[18]

The immigrant also had an opportunity, under the Homestead Act of 1862, to acquire free land; prior to 1890, over 48,000,000 acres were distributed. Between 1890 and 1933, over 185,000,000 additional acres were granted. Once settled on new claims, life was hard and money scarce, but the independent peasant background of many immigrants had prepared them for the struggle.

Land was also made available by the railroads in the years following the Civil War. Since it was in the interest of all rail companies to move people west, they sold much of the 127,628,000 acres of land given them by Congress, offering easy credit terms and agricultural guidance to interested settlers.

Today, land is not readily available to the poor. Farming is no remedy for the ills of the black man. Agriculture is fast becoming big business. Machines have replaced workers. While in 1900 a third of America's labor force were farmers or farm workers,[19] in 1967 farmers comprised but 4.3 per cent of the total work force.[20]

Furthermore, the immigrant often tends to forget that he was goaded on by the proverbial success story, by the Horatio Algers in his era, by the possibility of limitless upward mobility. There were so many ways to hit—through ingenuity, through hard work, or even through marriage. Such success tales and the optimism they engendered have always been virtually absent from the black community. In the first place, the black man who knew the South knew that ". . . aggressiveness in a Negro immediately brought him under suspicion." So did ambition. "The Southern Negro with thrift and ambition who began to move up in the world brought the envy of his white neighbors upon him, and exposed himself to danger."[21] Even when resettled in the North, this was a lesson hard to forget.

Secondly, there were special hurdles obstructing black progress. The would-be Negro businessman met "unbending prejudice and discrimination" in his attempts to get "stock, capital, or space for rent."[22] The worker was always underpaid yet had to pay more for less in housing, food and clothing. And, as Conot points out, the hard-working Negro boy just didn't make it with the white boss' daughter!

Bayard Rustin advises those who feel that "self help" is the answer for the Negro to look at the "long history" of such efforts. He points out that it isn't lack of motivation that keeps ". . . so many . . . on the shoals of ghetto life."

Negro youths have no need of statistics to perceive, fairly accurately, what their odds are in American society. Indeed, from the point of view of motivation, some of the healthiest Negro youngsters I know are juvenile delinquents: vigorously pursuing the American dream of material acquisition and status, yet finding the conventional means of attaining it blocked off, they do not yield to defeatism but resort to illegal (and often ingenious) methods. They are not alien to American culture. . . . To want a Cadillac is not un-American; to push a cart in the garment center is.[23]

Finally, the immigrant often overlooks the fact that his educational and familial backgrounds differ markedly from those of the American Negro. While the American system of slavery cut the Negro off from an education, the people who were someday to leave Europe for American shores were learning to read and write and were developing skills and traditions which would be helpful in later employment. Jewish parents instilled in their children the importance of attaining a good education in order to insure success in a world which discriminates against minorities. Germans learned lessons of industry and thrift. Greeks were growing up in an atmosphere that encouraged and rewarded individualism. In Ireland future immigrants were developing the know-how and discipline required for strong political organizations.

Similarly, in many European countries family ties and relationships were cemented early. In Italy divorce, separation and desertion were social stigmas; close, active family life was considered the norm for everyone. A well-defined pattern of authority existed, with the oldest male making decisions affecting all family members. Greek families, by and large, were close; roles were well defined with the father at the helm. The Irish, too, had close family ties and relationships.

In these societies and others where family closeness became a cultural goal children usually learned what their roles were and what they would become. A certain personal security was gleaned as they learned that they were both loved and needed. Pride in family life and pride in self were learned early as were the rewards that stability, devotion, and morality could bring.

Yet the Negro in America was forceably deprived of this experience. Purposefully, in many instances, the father was sold in one town, the mother in another, the children still elsewhere, and separately. This was the first step toward making the Negro slave totally dependent on the white man. By instituting an ingenious system which rewarded the slave who turned in a fellow slave for wrongdoing, the black man learned, too, that he could not even depend on his partners in oppression. The system ordained that loyalty was to move upward, not across to family or friends. Bonds of trust between blacks were never formed. Suspicion took their place.

Illegitimacy for Negroes was also institutionalized by the white man in the antebellum South. Because every new slave meant the production of more work, the increase of property, and the aggrandizement of wealth, most white slaveholders naturally encouraged childbirth. Yet, they didn't want their own positions jeopardized, so they refused to legalize slave marriages. The result was that marriage contracts between slaves were not legally binding. The North Carolina Supreme Court ruled that a marital relationship between slaves was ". . . essentially different from that of man and wife joined in lawful wedlock" because ". . . with slaves it may be dissolved at the pleasure of either party, or by the sale of one or both, depending upon the caprice or necessity of the owners."[24] Stampp points out that "in law there was no such thing as fornication or adultery between slaves; nor was there bastardy, for, as a Kentucky judge noted, the father of a slave was 'unknown' to the law."[25]

The natural and expected consequence was the reproduction of children without the benefit of marriage, a new and different morality, the further emasculation of the black male, and an alienated, sometimes resented, hungry, uncomprehending child. That these patterns of life still exist is little wonder, for the Negro took his past with him when he headed North to the big city ghetto and his past only began in the mid-1600's with slavery. He knew no other way of life, nor was he acquainted with or could he understand middle-class morality.

Because the immigrant had ties to, and pride in, family and clan, the newcomer to America could expect help from his brethren who had arrived earlier and had already begun their fight and their ascent. Not so the Negro migrant. He was ". . . largely ignored by his own people. The Negro who has made it and adopted white values does not want, by associating himself with lower caste members of his race, to be reminded of his Negroness."[26] With no pride in what he is, with only white-taught distrust of all that is black, it is little wonder that he has helped to poison his own.

There is no other group of people which came to this country with a background even closely similar to the hyphenated, turbulent, volatile background of the Negro. No other group was so greatly victimized, so torn asunder. It is not foolish to conclude that had the black man's heritage been different, the problems in the black ghettos—illegitimacy, broken homes and families, distrust of education—would hardly be as severe as they are today. And were his ghetto not so "dark," he would have been invited, or allowed, to drink of middle-class life in meaningful numbers.

4

The Perpetuation of the Ghetto

> I know there are white folk who want America to be the land of the free and the home of the brave, but there are far too few of them and most of them are seldom brave.[1]
>
> —JOHN KILLENS

There was nothing natural about the black man becoming a slave in America, the colonists' heritage of British subjugation in the black colonies, the world's tradition of white domination over black notwithstanding. For the country's earliest settlers had a dream—a dream that took shape against a background of, and in convulsingly violent reaction to, the British tradition of oppression and tyranny, the world's unchristian, inhumane practices. And it was that dream of freedom, that hope of equality, that carried them across an antagonistic ocean to a land which could offer the most basic of comforts only after years of ceaseless toil. They faced hardships that could be tempered only by the knowledge that their raw hands were building freedom and tolerance into the earth.

So while it may have been natural from a world view, or in historical perspective, for the system of slavery to grow in America, it was most unnatural in juxtaposition to the specific principles and ideals upon which the country was founded. Yet, basic principles were compromised early; freedom and opportunity were guaranteed only to some Americans.

In the beginning then, the idealists did not have enough faith in their own social, political and economic system—in their own ideals—to allow them to operate for all. They decided quickly to withhold from some the things they sought for themselves. In this unnatural fashion, they subverted their own goals by looking back into history and picking up one institution that made the new democracy a sham.

Must not the strains of racism run deep in that country which claims to be a democracy yet which subjugates black men? America's racist underpinnings became more structured as time went on and the institution of slavery became more formalized. In the South, legislation eventually gave official sanction to unjust practices and customs. In the North, practice and custom filled the void that resulted from an absence of legislation. With or without legal sanction, the black race was put on a one-way path that moved away from whites.

While the country today seems more aware of its internal inconsistencies as it faces its greatest identity crisis ever, it goes on mouthing promises as it kills dreams. In spite of the passage of Civil Rights Acts, in spite of heralded Supreme Court decisions, the world's most powerful democracy evidences strong racist strains. It is those strains which today undercut the Negro's ability to get anywhere in America. It is those strains which perpetuate the ghetto and the ghetto mentality.

WHAT IS PROGRESS?

The nation's desire to keep the races apart, the black race down, is nowhere more apparent than in the simple way in which America defines progress for the Negro. Progress is charted against the Negro's former position in society. Does he earn more than he used to earn? Is he better educated than he was? Does he have more playgrounds in his neighborhoods? Are there more black secretaries now, more black teachers than there were a decade ago?

It is significant that Negro advances are rarely compared to white advances when charts are drawn. This, for two reasons. First, because such a comparison could not assuage the guilt of policy-makers. Second, and more important, because the white man is not really interested in equalizing opportunity, nor in closing the gap between black and white. His interest, at best, is in making it possible for the Negro to escape some of the more aggravating and more tumultuous problems of life.

Bill Berry, a Chicago Urban League executive, enjoys telling about a meeting he attended. The subject was the ferment in Chicago's black community; the participants were influential Chicago businessmen and officials.

One of the businessmen, a gentleman who had worked hard to improve ghetto conditions, was upset about the area's restiveness: "Haven't we worked hard to do something? Hasn't the Negro made progress? Why is he pressuring so? What does he want?"

Bill sat back, smiled inwardly and answered, "Oh, he doesn't really want much. All he wants is what you have!"

"Oh," said his questioner, "I didn't know he wanted all that."

Whites aren't yet ready to fight for equal results and equal access. Equal opportunity? Maybe.

That America wishes to continue its unofficial policy of separation is further proven by the discrepancies between its words and actions. Such discrepancies pervade our national life and contribute directly to the perpetuation of the ghetto.

The Civil Rights Act of 1964, passed one hundred and one years after the abolishment of slavery, appeared to have considerable meaning for the future of the country, and the future of the black man. Yet this piece of legislation has reached neither to the heart of the problem nor to that segment of the population which suffers most. Despite the existence of Title VII, which provides for the elimination of discrimination in employment, broad patterns of discrimination can still be found in government, big and small business, and labor organizations.

The Equal Employment Opportunity Commission which administers Title VII is empowered to hold hearings or to negotiate and attempt to conciliate complaints it receives. If conciliation fails, it has no power to force companies to discontinue discriminatory practices.

Title VI states that

> No person in the United States shall, on the ground of race, color, or national origin, be excluded from participation in, be denied the benefits of, or be subjected to discrimination under any program or activity receiving Federal financial assistance.[2]

Each agency offering financial assistance is called upon to issue "rules, regulations, or orders of general applicability which shall be consistent with achievement of the objectives of the statute. . . . The failure to comply can result in the termination of Federal financial assistance."

Under this Title, the Department of Health, Education and Welfare, for example, is empowered to cut off Federal funds from those school districts which discriminate against Negro youngsters in Federally financed programs. To this day, HEW's Office of Civil Rights is involved in ceaseless quibbling over the wording of its regulations and the types and numbers of districts it should cite for noncompliance with the law. This, when more than 87 per cent of the black youngsters in the South were in segregated classrooms during the 1966-67 school year.[3]

The law clearly states that no person shall be discriminated against in Federally assisted programs. Yet, in administering Title VI, the Office of Education immediately interpreted the law to mean that if a school district discriminates a little less against a few, it can continue to discriminate against a great many. Indeed, the regulations were such that many districts which actually met the standards were still able to keep a dual school system operating.

This was bad enough, but with the coming of each new school year, the Office built up hopes in the Negro communities, only to dash them months later. Each spring and summer the Office of Education sent its official representatives through the South to explain the new guidelines for school desegregation, to tell school officials what they had to do in order to comply with the law. Then, in most cases, the Office failed to proceed against districts which did not meet the standards laid out just a few months earlier. Even districts which failed to comply with specific rules, like that against intimidation of Negro families exercising freedom of choice, were not punished.

The Office earlier adopted a policy or a strategy which it still both practices and defends. It deals most stringently with those districts it feels are easiest to "crack"—the districts with the smallest Negro populations. The larger the black school population in a city or town, the less likely that HEW will take action, regardless of the district's progress or lack of it. Indeed, those districts which are over 50 per cent black and totally segregated are put in a special category and are, for the most part, exempt from enforcement proceedings.

This is all the illusion—not the reality—of change. If after passing legislation, the Congress and the country allow governmental agencies to flirt away gains in further compromise, to what avail, laws?

That the reader might see and understand the extent of the damage that racism has perpetrated on the black citizen of America, three general areas need be studied—employment, housing and education. These three areas were chosen because they are the most crucial for the black man barred up in the ghetto. An analysis of problems in other areas, such as health, welfare and recreation, would undoubtedly yield parallel findings.

"...A MAN WITH A JOB"

It has been said that a recession is when your neighbors are out on the streets looking for work and a depression is when you're forced to join them. For a large segment of the Negro population, a perpetual cycle of depression is daily, monthly, and yearly fare. At any one time in the Negro ghetto areas of our major cities, there is an unemployment rate ranging from 10 to 25 per cent—an ugly statistic that has fluctuated little over the past eight to ten years. If American society generally approached such a high rate of unemployment, there would be chaos and upheaval.

The Department of Labor has shown that a Negro high school graduate has a greater chance of being unemployed than a white high school dropout.[4] Rashi Fein, a senior staff member at the Brookings Institution, has shown that a black student who attended, but did not finish, college earns less than a white student who completed but eight years of elementary school.[5] Phillip Hauser cites evidence that the more education a black man has, the greater the discrepancy between his earning capacity and that of a white man with similar training. The Negro with an occupational or educational background paralleling that of a white man receives lower wages. Negro carpenters with high school diplomas earn only 76 per cent of what white carpenters with the same diplomas earn.[6]

In 1964, in the three major pay systems of the Federal Government, Negroes held a much greater proportion of low paying jobs than high paying ones. Similarly, the proportion of workers in the lowest pay categories was greatest among Negroes. Under the Classification Act pay system, about 60 per cent of the Negroes were at the four lowest grade levels, as compared with 30 per cent of the whites. Under the Wage Board system, a third of all Negro workers earned under $4,500 compared with one-twelfth of the other employees.[7]

If the Negro's higher unemployment rate and his high concentration in blue-collar work are combined with the fact that opportunities for blue-collar workers and laborers are on the decline, one gets a realistic picture not only of the present depressed conditions of Negro employment but also of an even more bleak outlook for the future.

Impeding progress in the realization of equal employment opportunity and halting most attempts to change the inadequacies of a decadent, unjust system are barriers which America is still working hard to preserve.

The first is the phenomenon of the Negro job. White America magnanimously offers positions to Negroes that it would rather not perform itself. It willingly and graciously opens up such avenues as garbage collection, elevator operation, janitorial services and farm labor to its black brothers. These are conveniently the jobs in which the pay is lowest, the work is hardest and hottest, and employment tenure is the most tenuous. Promotions are rare, for higher rungs on the ladder—should they exist at all—are strictly off-limits to black feet. In addition, minimum wage regulations often do not apply. It is not solely for want of training that there is an amazingly disproportionate number of Negroes in these fields. It is not solely for want of ability that 76 per cent of the Negro male workers in poverty areas of the U.S. are employed as operatives, laborers, or service workers—jobs which are decreasing in size and significance as the economy continues to develop and expand.[8]

By keeping blacks in competition with other blacks, the power structure lets Negroes do to each other what it wants done. Someone once said that members of the Negro community are comparable to crabs enclosed in a basket. They scramble around together, clutching hold of each other. When one tries to rise to the top, another reaches up and pulls him back down. When such a situation has been set up, when so little is made available for so many, whites need not even clamp down a lid. If left to their own devices, Negroes will destroy each other as they fight for the few available rewards.

A closely related problem is that Negroes have very little job security as compared with whites, a fact brought out so well on "House Party" one day when Art Linkletter interviewed three little girls about age ten. He asked each one what kind of man she'd like to marry. The first white girl said that she would like to marry a man who works in a bank because he'd handle lots of money every day. The second girl, also white, said she wants to marry a man who works in an office, who carries a briefcase and wears a suit, a white shirt and a tie. The third little girl, a Negro, said that she wants to marry a man with a job.

If a school girl, still in her tender years, is already so preoccupied with the whole question of economic security, how burdened must adult minds be? The Negro feels insecure, even when employed, because the axiom "the last hired, the first fired" is as true today as it was the day it was coined. White America rewards those who have worked the longest before those who work best. The Negro, coming last, is thus the most vulnerable. Therefore, he lives on the verge of recession, if not in the midst of depression, all his life.

The result? The Negro can seek no adventure, nor can he afford to take any risks. He jumps on a merry-go-round and grabs the first horse he sees. He can't afford to be choosy—he might be left with none. He climbs on and clings to the animal for fear he will be thrown off. Around and around he rides, slowly getting nowhere. Yet, he dare not get off, for at least he is moving.

A third barrier to Negro employment is the employer's reluctance to hire Negroes at their highest skill levels. And, according to the report issued by the National Advisory Commission on Civil Disorders, ". . . underemployment is an even more serious problem for ghetto residents than unemployment."[9] Yet, many a black man has been forced to accept employment at a level far below that which his education and training would merit. I knew a young man who graduated first in his class in chemistry who is one case in point—there are thousands of others. He applied for a job as a chemist in an Ohio company and was told there were no jobs for chemists. Ray knew chemists were being hired, for the company had "talent scouts" roaming the country. But Ray wasn't a pusher. He was a quiet and studious man who was not trying to change the course of race relations. All he wanted was a job doing what he loved. So he didn't fight; he decided to go to graduate school at night, working days in the company as an elevator operator. But even with his advanced degree, no job.

I queried the company vice-president, asking why a man with a master's degree in chemistry was running an elevator in the company. "Does the company discriminate?"

"Oh, no," protested the vice-president, "we have no policy against hiring a Negro."

"But do you have a policy *for* it?"

He obviously didn't. And in the absence of policy, practice became policy.

Negroes with liberal arts college degrees and no specific technical skill run an even greater risk. The number of Negroes with college and advanced degrees working in routine jobs in the U. S. Post Office would astound even the most knowledgeable of liberals. The National Alliance of Postal Employees, an organization of Negro postal workers, is compiling a survey on the educational backgrounds of its new members. Although the survey is as yet incomplete, the Alliance has found that of those who have returned the questionnaire indicating they have college degrees, over 75 per cent hold jobs as clerks or carriers. The President of the National Alliance himself, with a law degree from the University of Chicago Law School, came to his present position from a job as clerk in the Post Office Department.

The lack of upward mobility compounds the Negro's already crippling burden. It is no secret that black men don't get promoted as quickly as white men. Indeed, many workers can never move up at all. Consequently, the Negro employee is stripped of the most important ingredient in the free enterprise system, incentive.

I addressed a group of businessmen in Warren, Ohio, some years back on the subject of opening up job opportunities to Negroes. One man who was moved by the discussion invited me to come and see his plant. As we walked up and down the aisles, we saw Negroes working with brooms, white men working on machines. Some Negroes were working hard, others were standing around going through the motions. As a group, they didn't exactly form a picture of industriousness. Almost all the white men, on the other hand, were working zealously.

The plant owner looked around and said he'd like to give the Negro an equal opportunity, but he couldn't because his is a highly competitive business and if he put Negroes on machines, production would slow down and he'd be forced out of business.

This reasoning surprised me and I asked how the machine operators and the janitors were paid. I was told that the machinists got paid for each piece of work they turned out, and that they recieved a bonus for each piece over a certain number. The janitors, on the other hand, got a flat weekly salary.

I then pointed out that no man will work hard if he is handed a broom, told to sweep, and is shown that no matter how fast and hard he pushes the broom, he'll never be anything but a janitor. "Don't confuse the symptom with the problem here. The problem is not color, it is *incentive* as you'll see if you put Negroes on machines and relegate whites to moving brooms around."

Keeping large numbers of prospective Negro employees from securing employment is an array of evaluative devices that are middle-class oriented. Such devices rarely measure how well one can perform on a given job, but rather present a picture of how well the applicant has mastered verbal and arithmetic skills and digested cultural information—skills in which the black ghetto resident is admittedly deficient due to a weak and often meager education, an alienation from middle-class values and culture. Such tests might have validity if the job in question required math or the mastery of the English language or culture. Many don't, yet witness some sample questions similar to those building-trades artisans must answer:

Czolgosz is to Booth as McKinley is to ....

A. Lincoln B. Washington C. Roosevelt D. Garfield

Aztec is to Mexico as Maya is to ....
A. Peru B. Guatemala C. Haiti D. Uruguay

.... is to phlegmatic as vivacious is to ....
1. husky 2. rheumatic 3. pneumatic 4. sluggish
A. elusive B. pouting C. exuberant D. gripping[10]

Thomas O'Hanlon was right:

For reasons known only to themselves, the unions [building trades] have chosen to select aptitude tests heavily weighted in favor of verbal sophistication and an intimate understanding of white middle-class culture. In addition, the potential plumbers, electricians, sheet-metal workers, and other building-trades artisans are required to possess a range of cultural and literary information wholly inappropriate to success in these crafts.[11]

Another question, this from the Wonderlic Personnel Test, used by a large number of Washington, D.C., employers. This question actually penalizes the man from the lower-class environment.

Suppose you arranged the following words so that they made a true statement. Then print the last letter of the last word as the answer to this problem.

than fortunate rich be better[12]

The creators of the test deem the true statement to be "Better be fortunate than rich." But, they are middle-class. Drawing on a wealth of personal experience, many a lower-class slum dweller feels that "Better be rich than fortunate" is the true statement. But test evaluators care little what the ghetto culture teaches. The ghetto's answer is wrong by their standards. There can be but one "right" answer!

Many civil rights and human relations groups have waged little wars against the standardized test in an attempt to prove their lack of validity in employment situations. The Urban League's on-the-job training staff has offered assistance to job applicants slated to take the Wonderlic. Staff personnel administered a test similar to the Wonderlic. After the test was completed, it was discussed with the applicant and methods of handling multiple-choice questions were studied. The applicant then reported to the employer's office and took the test. In most cases, individuals whose trial test scores did not meet employer requirements passed the test the second time.

League officials, however, feel that they've won but a minor victory even though they've won their point, because industry and government refuse to change the standards of job qualification. A person seeking a job as a multilith operator for the government must take and pass the Civil Service Office Assistant examination. The test consists of vocabulary, grammar, spelling, word relations, reading and math. Yet, according to the government's own *Dictionary of Occupational Titles,* a multilith operator

> operates offset-duplicating machine to reproduce single or multicolor copies of charts, schedules, bulletins, and related matter . . . installs sensitized metal printing plate or master copy of plastic-coated paper around press cylinder of machine and locks plate or master copy into position, using handtools. Turns handwheel and ink fountain screws to regulate ink flow. Selects paper stock to be printed according to color, size, thickness, and quantity specified, stacks paper on feed table, and positions spring guide on side of paper stack. Turns elevator crank to raise feed table to paper height. Sets dial controls to adjust speed and feed of machine according to weight of paper. Starts machine. . . . Cleans and files master copy of plate. Cleans and oils machine. . . .[13]

In one community, the telephone company claimed it was seeking Negro operators. Many women applied; large numbers failed the qualifying examination. An Urban League official got permission to examine some of the tests and found that there was generally weak performance on the vocabulary sections. In talking with company officials, he pointed out that a large vocabulary seemed irrelevant since operators, in their training, are taught about a dozen canned sentences. For most questions, there is a prepared answer which the operator is trained to give. She is expected to say little else.

A closely related problem which works to the detriment of the Negro is the requirement of college and other advanced degrees for jobs that could well be performed with less academic training. A government economist with a master's degree once told me that he never had a job that a high school graduate with a good education couldn't perform, given some limited instruction. The ability to collect degrees does not guarantee the ability to produce anyway; a lack of degrees does not indicate the inability to produce.

The labor market in this country is in a state of perpetual flux. New kinds of jobs are always developing and new opportunities continue to appear, but such jobs cannot be landed by the man who is unskilled and untrained. The unskilled worker is becoming an increasingly unneeded commodity on the labor scene. And the unskilled worker is, one time out of four, a black man.[14]

Training programs have yet to become meaningful. They have yet to hit the hard core unemployed.[15] Were the Labor Department to turn a whole segment of its operation, at the local and national level, into a massive university for remediation, offering a plethora of training programs, restricted at first to those out of work and next to those whose skills are becoming less marketable, the government could pride itself on a good beginning.

To date, the government and private industry have not built sufficient incentives into their training programs. In fact, they have often made it impossible for some job seekers to enter the program by charging fees, because even a minimal fee of three or five dollars is more than an unemployed man with a family of four or five can afford. There has been little released time for training. Government and private employers have been loath to give time off to unskilled workers during the work week to attend classes. Government has yet to offer to pay the salaries of workers whom industry will not qualify and pay to enter its training programs. Perhaps the greatest shortcoming of the training programs offered to date has been the false hopes they have raised because they are not always tied to jobs or promotions.

Discrimination in the trade unions does irreparable damage to the black worker. And, while discrimination is greatest in the building trades, it exists in most unions. Negroes are now allowed to trickle in so that unions can prove they don't discriminate, but the funnel is narrow and most black workers are kept out. The system is an ingenious one, designed first to discriminate and then to hide the evidence. Barrier number one is the apprenticeship training program from which most Negroes are barred. He who manages to serve as an apprentice gets his name added to the union waiting list. Lists are long and their mere existence makes discrimination hard to prove. In Washington, D.C., where building is the city's second largest industry, it took efforts from the Vice-President, the Secretary of Labor, the head of the AFL-CIO, the General Services Administration and the President's Committee on Equal Employment Opportunity to get one Negro electrician a job working on a government building in the early 1960's.

Government has yet to force compliance by refusing to contract out its programs to those industries that won't use 5 to 10 per cent of their on-the-job training funds for Negroes. It has yet to limit its business to contractors who subcontract only with integrated unions. Labor unions have yet to organize Negroes in meaningful numbers, have yet to negotiate equal wages for those it has organized. Herman P. Miller of the Bureau of the Census estimates that Negro factory workers nationally earn 32 per cent less than whites, while black truck drivers and delivery men earn 42 per cent less than whites. Dr. Vivian Henderson, President of Clark College, studied twenty-seven job categories in "traditionally unionized industries" outside the South and found that in twenty-six of these categories, nonwhites earned considerably less than whites—the twenty-seventh category was bus drivers.[16]

Even organized crime, which finds a profitable home in the black ghetto, discriminates against Negroes. Jewish, Italian, and Irish gangsters tend to favor their own when it comes to hiring and promoting. And underworld customs being what they are, it is more than a little risky for any Negro to buck the Establishment and try to make it on his own.

The enterprising Negro who manages to gain entrance into the underworld must resign himself to a "blue-collar" job—errand boy, narcotics peddler, numbers runner. As a Boston loan shark put it: "Most of the Big Boys don't want them in responsible positions. You need people you can be sure about in this business. You feel better with your own kind, you know what I mean?"[17]

However dismal the job picture for the black adult male, it is even more hopeless for the black youth, the black female not willing to be a maid, or the black with a police record.

In March 1966, the unemployment rate in poverty areas was 45.8 per cent for nonwhite girls aged fourteen to nineteen and 30.6 per cent for nonwhite boys. The rate of unemployment for all Negro teen-agers was 11.5 per cent or nearly three times the rate of all workers. Female unemployment in slum areas reached 8.1 per cent in 1966—more than twice that of the national unemployment rate.[18]

The ex-convict, generally, has great difficulty obtaining a job because many employers are afraid to take a risk and hire him. He is generally denied employment because of his record, regardless of the cause of the record. It is often of no consequence whether he looted, robbed or knifed, or whether he was only arrested and never convicted.

The Negro ex-convict has perhaps been punished most by America's moralistic immoral system because he faces double discrimination—first for his record, then for his color. Society emblazons a scarlet letter on his chest and sends him out in the streets to compete. He has little chance for success. If he wants money or food, he must steal it. What a strange lesson for a society to teach!

Little interest has been shown at any level of the official world in the problem of the ex-convict. One of the two exciting programs in the Washington, D.C., area for ex-cons has had difficulty getting government money to continue its invaluable operations.

Bon-a-bond and EFEC (Effort From Ex-Convicts) work to help the ex-convict help himself move back into society. Both are selective membership organizations run by ex-convicts themselves. Bon-a-bond is very proud of the fact that most of its staff positions can be filled only by ex-convicts. The organization seeks employment for new members, assists narcotics addicts who want to kick the habit, and sponsors convicts who are released into its custody. EFEC similarly develops self-help programs for its members in employment and community service and also attempts to enlighten the society and improve the image of ex-convicts generally. Both programs have successfully placed large numbers of men and women in jobs.

The Watts Manufacturing Company is also proving that ex-convicts are good work risks. More than half its workers have police records, yet supervisors, who have had experience in other concerns, report that the pilferage rate is "remarkably lower" than at other companies where a police record is a bar to employment.

NOT JUST BRICK AND MORTAR

The contrast between life inside the ghetto and life on the outside is stark, especially in the area of housing. In the state of California, about half of the nonwhites who rent and two-fifths of the nonwhites who are homeowners live in substandard housing units. By comparison, only one-fifth of the white renters and one-tenth of the white homeowners are in substandard units.[19] A large percentage of Los Angeles' Negroes live in the Watts area in conditions which are three times as crowded and congested as conditions in other parts of the city.[20] The statistics become tediously and alarmingly repetitive as each new American city is studied. In Harlem, 44 per cent of the housing units have been labeled *slum* by the city of New York.[21] In 1965, there were more than one hundred people per acre, and nearly half of the units had been built before 1900.[22] In Chicago, in 1964, most Negroes lived in ghetto areas and paid about twenty dollars more each month per family for housing than their white equivalents.[23] In Cleveland, in 1960, when Negroes represented 32 per cent of all renters in the city, they occupied 42 per cent of all substandard units, 55 per cent of the overcrowded units, and 45 per cent of the units costing more than a fourth of the total family income.[24]

The national picture is no more comforting. In 1960, 30 per cent of the nation's nonwhite housing units had no bathtubs or showers, 41 per cent of the nonwhite units either had no bathrooms or shared bathrooms, 20 per cent had no piped water, and only 75 per cent had flush toilets.[25] In addition, 3.7 per cent of the white families with incomes of ten thousand dollars a year or over lived in substandard housing, while 15 per cent of the nonwhite families with similar incomes inhabited substandard dwellings[26] And, according to a bulletin issued by the United States Department of Labor:

> Of the 16,836,000 housing units added to the "standard housing" supply, between 1950 and 1960, almost 9 in 10 went to white occu-

pants. In that period the number of white-occupied substandard units dropped by 50 per cent compared to less than a 20 per cent decline in non-white-occupied substandard units.[27]

There is simply not enough decent housing available to Negroes. During World War II, the housing industry practically came to a standstill. It was one of the many nonessential industries that was a war casualty. When the war ended, the country was faced with the expected housing shortage, exacerbated by a baby boom and the sharply increased cost of labor. Given the steep labor costs, it became too expensive for the private housing industry to build to the need market. It could not afford to build low income housing, as there was no profit in it. Indeed, there was loss.

For about twenty years, the country did little to cope with the resulting problem, the lack of adequate housing facilities for the poor. For many years, community after community rejected the concept of public housing. In Seattle, Washington, for example, public housing opponents in 1950 waged a successful campaign to defeat a local referendum. They labeled public housing a "road to socialism." Ads appeared in the local papers; one depicted a cartoon character labeled "Public Housing" whose arm was outstretched as he greeted a homeowner and taxpayer, remarking, "I've come to collect *your* half of *my* rent!"[28]

Similar smear-like tactics were used elsewhere with identical results. Thus, cities like Racine, Wisconsin, Grand Rapids, Michigan, St. Paul, Minnesota, St. Louis, Missouri, Rapid City, South Dakota and Portland, Oregon, all voted down public housing measures.

Some thirteen states adopted legislation requiring a referendum before public housing projects could be started. This was a dilatory tactic that often halted the offensive. Many localities were forced to leave temporary war barracks intact to house their poor. Others refused to blight their streets with these eyesores and tore them down, even though they were needed, building nothing to replace them.

After World War II, the private housing industry built where there was the most profit. The consequence was an abundance of middle- and upper-income housing dwellings in suburbs that were off-limits to blacks. The government, in typical myopic fashion, aggravated the worsening social problem by abetting the construction of all-white suburbs. A 1938 directive in FHA's own Underwriting Manual read: "If a neighborhood is to retain stability, it is necessary that properties shall continue to be occupied by the same social and racial group."[29] This directive was overtly operative throughout the 1940's. It is covertly operative today, for the Agency continues to do business with builders, lenders and real estate brokers who discriminate and thereby keep the Negro confined to the ghetto.

Government-financed urban renewal projects are further strangling the black man. Sixty to 72 per cent of the people displaced by urban renewal have been Negro, while only a small number of new homes and apartments built on black land have been open for reoccupancy to black people.[30] Washington, D.C.'s, famed Southwest area is a good example. Southwest was once considered the shame of the nation's capital. Located three blocks from the Capitol and ten blocks from the White House, it was as recently as 1957 an "overcrowded, incredibly primitive" and predominantly Negro slum, housing 23,500 people, approximately 77 per cent of them black.

Today, the area is highly modernistic with broad avenues, majestic, carpeted apartment buildings, luxurious townhouses and new, bright, modern stores. The area now houses upwards of 14,000 people, around 15 to 18 per cent of them black.

But even these shocking figures don't tell the full story, because before urban renewal, approximately 81 per cent of Southwest's population had an income under $4,800 a year. Today, while income figures are not readily available, the rentals in the area indicate that a substantial income is required for Southwest living—the rents range from $114 a month for an efficiency unit to $410 a month for a three-bedroom penthouse. Townhouses can be purchased for $29,260 and up. There is no low-income housing in the renewal area itself, except for 107 units operated by St. James Mutual Homes, a rehabilitation cooperative.

The urban renewal process in Southwest Washington uprooted a total of more than 23,000 poor people. More than 4,000 homes were razed.

The housing industry is perhaps more dependent on government than any other nondefense segment of industry in the economy. Without government support, the industry would go out of business. Government's leverage is, consequently, exceedingly great. Yet, despite government's potential power, there remains more discrimination in housing than anywhere else. In the late fifties, only 4 of 32 Chicago suburban jurisdictions had over 100 nonwhites residing in them.[31] In 1967, a group of prominent Chicago residents found that of 2,000 homes listed for sale, only 38 were open to Negroes.[32] *The New York Times* recently reported that under 5 per cent of New York State's suburban population is nonwhite and that many of these nonwhites live together in slum pockets at the edge of new suburbs.[33] And in the Washington, D.C., metropolitan area, the home of the Federal Government, the home of the President, the American Friends Service Committee reports that as of June 1967 only 22 apartment buildings in suburban Maryland and Virginia were open to Negroes.[34] This number represents about one-tenth of 1 per cent of all the apartments in Washington suburbs.

Housing officials have for years built one mistake onto another, evidencing more interest in cementing together their errors than in undoing them. The result is a gargantuan network of miscalculation, urban monuments of failure.

Public housing was a good concept on paper. But, the high-paid planners failed to anticipate the problems which would result from high-rise, self-contained public housing communities. They didn't see that people living in such units would be stigmatized and that a psychology of failure would thus be built into every room. They also did not concentrate their efforts on ending segregation as they built; indeed, they reinforced it by building most public housing facilities in the center of cities, where whites no longer live. According to a report issued by the Civil Rights Commission in 1967:

> Of the quarter of a million public housing units that have been built by city public housing authorities in the Nation's 24 largest metropolitan areas, in only one, Cincinnati, has the city housing authority been permitted to build outside the central city. There the authority has provided a total of 76 low-rent units in the suburbs.[35]

It was no accident of fate that by 1967, about 70 per cent of all Federally assisted public housing units were occupied by members of one race.

America's leaders have consciously rejected, for the most part, the construction of mixed-income public housing, even in cities. And they have never used urban renewal as a tool to get people into the suburbs—they have opted to use it to lock people into the cities. The result has been the relocation of the poor from one ghetto to another larger, more crowded ghetto.

Integration, it seems, will be feasible only when low-income housing is built in every suburb, leaving whites no escape route. It may be impossible to build public housing communities in the suburbs, but it is not so difficult to build mixed-income private housing in each neighborhood and in each of the subdivisions that is constructed. And with government subsidies, the poor would be able to move in.

America did not even insure that its public housing network would come close to meeting the nation's needs. As Congressman Widnall pointed out in testimony before Senator Ribicoff's Subcommittee on Executive Reorganization in 1966, 35 per cent of the country's urban renewal funds could be used for commercial, nonresidential renewal.

> By the Department of Housing and Urban Development's own figures, in the past 5 years . . . projects have been approved that allocate 97 percent of the future funds for urban renewal in Atlanta to non-residential development. The figure is 77 percent for Baltimore, 62 percent for Boston, 60 percent for Chicago, 49 percent for Cleveland, 56 percent for New York City, and 75 percent for Philadelphia. Every dollar spent for non-residential renewal means that much less for our low-income citizen and our slum dweller.[36]

At the end of 1967, the National Capital Housing Authority reported that in Washington, D.C., alone, there was a waiting list of nearly 3,000 for public housing. New York City's Housing Authority listed over 100,000 people waiting for public housing; in Chicago, in February 1968, the number totaled over 20,000. These are people who have already met the standards and qualified for public housing; the number does not include the very low-income city dweller whose meager income labels him a high risk and, therefore, ineligible for public housing rolls.

That citizens have to qualify for public housing is cruel enough. Then to place more stock in the receipt of forms than in the consideration of humanity, especially of those about to lose their homes to bulldozers, is the height of man's inhumanity to man. Yet, the form game is played. The following appeared in an Urban League report:

> The documentary proof required of a public housing applicant was meticulous and enormously detailed. An applicant was required to supply: a birth certificate, a marriage license, a divorce decree (if any), income verification to be obtained from each employer, Social Security or other welfare payments certified by the respective agencies, verification of medical disabilities from all attending physicians or clinics, verification of expenditures for child care in case of working mothers, etc., etc. The applicant was to fill out or obtain all of these forms (in case of birth certificates from Southern states, often an impossible task); take time off his job to take them to the proper agencies for verification and to spend carfare for the trips to and from the agencies, often wait hours in line or sometimes days and months for an appointment. If medical verification was needed, the prospective applicant had to wait for his regular clinic appointment often scheduled months ahead at D.C. General or Freedmen's Hospitals, to assure the filling out of his forms. Meanwhile, his application for housing could not proceed, no matter how pressing his housing needs.[37]

Why has America done so little when the need is so great? Public housing is, in large part, Negro housing, and Congress hasn't wanted to subsidize Negro housing because there are not enough votes in it yet. Indeed, there is not enough power in the entire low-income population to make it an issue significant enough for Congress to do more than make a passing gesture at the consideration of its problems. It is hard to understand how the richest nation in the world can seem to feel no disgrace in having constructed only about 675,000 units of public housing in all of America when New York City alone needs 200,000 units just to house its low-income families presently living in grossly substandard dwellings.

According to the late Robert Kennedy, public housing is not, in itself, an answer to the problems of the ghetto.

Public housing was once thought of as *the* answer to the problems of slums. Therefore it became another of those programs, addressed to some symptomatic shortcoming, which has ignored the wider problem, the other needed government action. Our housing projects were built largely without either reference or relevance to the underlying problems of poverty, unemployment, social disorganization, and alienation which caused people to need assistance in the first place. Too many projects, as a result, became jungles—places of despair and danger for their residents, and for the cities they were designed to save. Many of them are preserved from this fate only by screening, such as is practiced in New York City, to keep the "problem" families—who of course are most in need of help—out of public housing projects, while families with incomes as high as $9,000 a year live there. And therefore, it has been, too often, a failure.[38]

As America built its concrete islands of isolation, it made no attempt to better the services offered ghetto residents, knowing all too well that the poor get the worst in all service areas. In Washington, D.C., teen-agers in special work programs had to clean up the mess remaining after the sanitation workers "finished." Commenting on sanitation problems in Boston's ghettos, Mrs. Pearl Lee told Civil Rights Commission investigators:

It does not take a genius to figure out that these streets haven't been swept in five or six months. When we lived on Beacon Street the street sweeper was there every morning with water and brushes.[39]

Taxi service can be hard to come by in San Francisco's black Potrero Hill section. As Robert Jacobs told the Commission:

. . . on certain occasions I have waited for something like four or five hours just to get a taxi to come four or five blocks with groceries for my family.

At one time I had sickness in my family and I tried to get a taxi. I had to pay an additional $35 just to get my child to the hospital, because the taxi said they couldn't find it and they didn't want to come out there.[40]

In the area of public transportation, even the McCone Commission found that

. . . the inadequate and costly public transportation currently existing throughout the Los Angeles area seriously restricts the residents of the disadvantaged areas. . . . This . . . handicaps them in seeking and holding jobs, attending schools, shopping, and in fulfilling other needs.[41]

Health-care facilities in the ghetto are inadequate, too. In Los Angeles, the McCone Commission found that

. . . there are 106 physicians for some 252,000 people, whereas the county ratio is three times higher. The hospitals readily accessible to the citizens in southeastern Los Angeles are also grossly inadequate in quality and in number of beds. . . . The two large public hospitals, County General and Harbor General, are both distant and difficult to reach.[42]

The Civil Rights Commission found in Cleveland that

. . . although the greatest health problems were concentrated in the East Side Negro areas, the only public hospital was located on the West Side.[43]

The fact that the ghetto gets the worst services is reason alone why isolation of the poor, isolation of the Negro, is unworkable. Indeed, one of the reasons Negroes want integration is that they know that it is the only way to insure getting the same facilities and services available to the white man. They know that when garbage collection gets cut back, it gets cut back in the black neighborhoods first. The Skelly Wright decision told them what they already knew, that the black schools in Washington, D.C., were the schools short-changed in facilities.[44] If this is the pattern of the American mind, the only way to escape is to change one's conditions if one is ghettoized and live where these conditions do not exist. That is why Negroes want to live near whites. Whites are going to get the best that America has to offer and blacks, too, wish to partake.

Ghettos are also strengthened by the decision not to build private low-income housing facilities. America builds for profit alone and the upper middle class reaps the benefits. Agencies like the FHA, which look on approvingly, become middle-class tools which support existing housing patterns. By its inaction, government has added more than its share to the deterioration of the inner city and the proliferation of ghettos.

Discrimination has been encouraged by some Federal housing programs. The FHA and the Veterans Administration together have financed over one hundred twenty billion dollars worth of new housing since World War II, yet less than 2 per cent of this housing has been available to nonwhites.[45] Only recently, eight Congressmen charged the FHA with following "a passive policy" toward enforcing President Kennedy's 1962 Executive Order which prohibits racial discrimination in housing sold under mortgages which are Federally insured. "It is well known that FHA's principal constituency is the housing industry. . . . FHA is reluctant to jeopardize its standing with the industry by aggressively implementing an equal opportunity policy."[46]

The Housing Assistance Administration, responsible for upwards of 600,000 dwellings in 2,000 American cities, admits that 70 per cent of its public housing projects are segregated. The National Committee against Discrimination in Housing claims 90 per cent is a more accurate figure.[47] The HAA claims it is making attempts to desegregate new housing projects, but as long as it permits local authorities to choose areas for construction, such efforts are doomed. The Renewal Assistance Administration, with programs in over 800 cities, could well promote desegregation by compelling local redevelopment agencies to relocate those Negroes who are displaced in white neighborhoods. However, with rare exceptions, its renewal techniques have aided the cause of segregation in that they have expanded ghettos.

The Department of Housing and Urban Development sponsors programs which deal with about 20 per cent of the new housing built every year, exclusive of the Model Cities and Rent Supplement programs. It determines procedures and policies in housing and related fields—its ". . . actions set up social currents which modify the manners and morals of the entire housing industry, from the great lending institutions to the small landlords."[48] According to the National Committee against Discrimination in Housing:

Nearly everything the Government touches turns to segregation, and the Government touches nearly everything. The billions of dollars it spends on housing, highways, hospitals and other community facilities are dollars that buy ghettos. Ditto for the billions the Government has given to American cities and suburbs in the name of community planning—money which made it simple for planners to draw their two-color maps and to plot the precise locations of Watts, Hough, Hunter's Point and ten thousand other ghettos across the land.[49]

The first federal fair housing law wasn't passed until 1968. Discrimination in the sale of housing wasn't declared unconstitutional by the Supreme Court until that year. Only twenty-one states have laws against it; three others have regulations limited to federal or state projects. Even with these laws, weak enforcement has militated against actual residential integration.

The result is that the demand for Negro housing is far in excess of supply, both in and out of the ghetto. Negroes compete with Negroes for the limited housing available and prices soar because it is a seller's market. Those who lose out in the competition for suburban homes remain in the ghetto. There are many! It is not only the poor who get sucked and locked in. In our capitalistic, materialistic, money-oriented society, not even a decent income can guarantee a black man a one-way trip out. As the Census Bureau reported at the end of 1967, over 50 percent of the black people in slum areas are there not because they are poor, but because of the rigid patterns of housing segregation. "Economic status alone does not explain the large proportion of nonwhite families in poverty areas."[50]

And, the numbers and percentages are increasing. Inner cities are becoming blacker; more and more whites are moving to the suburbs. In 1960, 10.3 million nonwhites—more than half of the country's nonwhite population—lived in central cities. This represented a gain of 63 per cent over 1950. In the nation's 212 standard metropolitan statistical areas in 1960, 52 per cent of the whites lived outside the central city whereas 78 per cent of the nonwhites lived within the central city.[51]

When Carl Rowan moved to Washington, D.C., to assume the post of Deputy Assistant Secretary of State for Public Affairs, he was able to purchase a home in a predominantly white area. One Saturday, Carl, dressed in old clothes, was out mowing the lawn when a lady in a chauffeur-driven limousine beckoned to him.

"How much do you get for mowing lawns?" she queried.

"Well," said Mr. Rowan, scratching his head, "well ma'am, I don't have a set price. As a matter of fact, I don't charge the lady in this house anything. She lets me sleep with her!"

How set and inflexible the patterns of residential segregation must be when a black man working on his lawn is immediately assumed to be the yard boy.

Where housing restrictions that limit black progress end, banking institutions and real estate boards take over. These establishments decide who will get credit and for what property. In Washington, most realtors discourage whites from buying in the District of Columbia while they keep Negroes from buying in the holy land west of Rock Creek Park. The same pattern can be found in any city. Thus, many members of the middle class whose incomes would otherwise enable them to break out of their constricting environments are unable to do so because they are black and thus subject to the special restrictions of unauthorized legislators.

Urban renewal efforts have been short-sighted, too. Generally, in the name of progress, renewal plans call for the tearing down of housing inhabited by those whose need for housing is greatest in order that middle- and upper-class dwellings can be built. Often, some low-income dwellings are constructed, but never enough to rehouse those displaced.

According to an official in HUD, 383,000 units had been demolished for urban renewal as of June 1967. In their place 107,000 units were constructed in renewal areas, less than 25 per cent of them for low-income residents. In addition, the mere announcement that an area has been selected for renewal imposes hardship on area residents. As the Urban League staff discovered in studying the Pierce Street renewal project in Washington, D.C.:

> After the area was designated for urban renewal, the real estate companies which owned the majority of the houses on the street made few repairs. Many of the houses had no heat, the walls were crumbling, ceilings were caving in, floor boards were full of holes. Yards and lots were taken over by weeds, and rats made the street their domain. Old furniture and trash littered the empty lots. The houses which stood empty attracted vagrants and armed gangs of youngsters. Drunks hung around the corner liquor store. . . .[52]

In the Hough district of Cleveland, Morris Thorington, a black businessman, testified in a Civil Rights Commission hearing that urban renewal was "urban destruction" because housing units slated for demolition still stood. "They are nothing but a meeting ground for hoodlums, prostitutes or what have you."[53] The deterioration of the neighborhood slated for renewal was, according to Commission staff,

> . . . traceable in part to the decision by local urban renewal officials several years earlier not to enforce the Cleveland Housing Code in Hough and other areas designated for renewal. Testimony revealed that one apparent reason for the decision to suspend code enforcement was the desire to keep property acquisition costs low.[54]

Never have housing officials attempted to stage urban renewal the way they would remodel a house—by moving into one part while they fix another, and moving into the new section while they remodel the old.

Relocation plans have also failed. All too often, people move out of an area when urban renewal is imminent and into housing far above their means for fear they'll be left with no shelter at all. No relocation assistance reaches them. Others turn down the option of moving back into the neighborhood when low-income housing is being constructed, not understanding their rights and wary of moving families across town and then back again. Housing experts haven't even begun to implement plans to construct temporary housing right in target neighborhoods. Yet, officials constructed temporary dwellings during World War II when housing was badly needed. Is the need of those to be evacuated out of a slum area any less acute today?

EDUCATION—STERILITYVILLE

The nation's inability to integrate its schools has caused incalculable damage to the American educational system, American children, and American society. If the Civil Rights Commission was correct in its recent study, *Racial Isolation in the Public Schools,* the performance, aspirations and attitudes of students are adversely affected by attendance in segregated classrooms. The Commission, drawing upon information presented in the

Office of Education's *Equality of Educational Opportunity* report, even goes further by concluding that

> . . . the performance of Negro students is distinctly less related to differences in the quality of schools and teachers than the social class and racial composition of their schools. This further reinforces the conclusion that the quality of education presently provided in schools does little to reverse the inequalities imposed upon children by factors within and outside the schools. The analysis thus suggests that changes in the social class or racial composition of schools would have a greater effect upon student achievement and attitudes than changes in school quality.[55]

Integration would be more beneficial than compensatory education programs.

We know that Negro students—be they advantaged or disadvantaged—perform better when they attend integrated schools. We know that the more time ". . . Negro students are in racially isolated schools, the greater the negative impact. . . ." We know conversely that there is ". . . a consistent trend toward higher academic performance for Negro students the longer they are in school with whites."[56] We also know that the society consistently views Negro schools as inferior and that teachers " 'average down' their expectations" of their students. And we know that racial isolation in schools fosters attitudes that perpetuate and intensify racial isolation in other phases of our national life.

We know all this, yet we persist. Today, the great majority of children in America attend schools that are "largely segregated." In 1967, the Civil Rights Commission concluded that "racial isolation in the schools . . . is intense whether the cities are large or small, whether the proportion of Negro enrollment is large or small, whether they are located North or South."[57]

The nation's highest Court has established the legal basis for school integration in a large number of cases. In 1938, in Gaines v. Canada, the Court ruled that a state is under obligation to provide its Negro residents the advantages of higher education substantially equal to the advantages afforded its white students. Refusing to do so constituted denial of equal protection of the laws. This ruling ended the state-financed annual Northern summer exodus of Negro students seeking degrees in higher education.

In a similar case, Sipuel v. the Board of Regents, University of Oklahoma, the state of Oklahoma was ordered to provide a legal education to qualified Negro applicants as soon as it did the applicants of other groups. The new emphasis here was on timing.

In Sweatt v. Painter, the Supreme Court ruled that it could not find ". . . substantial equality in the educational opportunities offered white and Negro law students by the State." It pointed to such things as the number of faculty members, variety of courses and opportunity for specialization to support its contention. In the Court's own words:

> What is more important, the University of Texas Law School possesses to a far greater degree those qualities which are incapable of objective measurement but which make for greatness in a law school. Such qualities . . . include reputation of the faculty, experience of the administration, position and influence of the alumni, standing in the community, traditions and prestige.[58]

The Court thus set a precedent by assessing the intangible qualities of a school and relating them to equal opportunity.

The Court also took into account intangible considerations in McLaurin v. Oklahoma State Regents. It ruled that a Negro admitted to a state graduate school is entitled to the same treatment by the state as other students; hence he could not be assigned to special places in the classroom, library or cafeteria or he would be deprived of the personal right to equal protection of the laws.

Whatever the Court left unsaid about separate but equal in these cases, it unequivocally stated in 1954 in Brown v. the Board of Education when it ruled that "the doctrine of 'separate but equal' " has no place in the field of public education since "separate educational facilities are inherently unequal." Chief Justice Warren went on to say that ". . . segregation of children in public schools solely on the basis of race, even though the physical facilities and other 'tangible' factors may be equal, deprive the children of the minority group of equal educational opportunities. . . ."[59]

If one agrees that it is all right to separate on the basis of color, one acknowledges that there is a difference because of color alone. Why else separation based upon color? If one agrees that there is a difference based upon color, he is saying, in effect, that one color is better than another. He is further saying that the government of the United States recognizes that difference. The Brown decision of 1954 points out that the government of the United States does not and cannot recognize difference based upon color.

Separate but equal is unjust because inherent in the concept of separation is a recognition of a difference which would justify the separation; then in effect, inequality results. Thus, the only way to guarantee that Negro children get the same education white children get is to insure that they are in the same classroom at the same time with the same teacher getting the same information.

It would appear a logical next step that if *de jure* segregation must be eliminated to insure Negro youngsters an equal educational opportunity, then *de facto* segregation must be eliminated to accomplish the same purpose, because the effects of de facto segregation are just as invidious as the effects of de jure segregation. The Brown decision has yet to be interpreted in this way; but it must be, for the problem is the condition of segregation, whatever its cause.

The Skelly Wright decision in the Hobson v. Hansen case in the District of Columbia brings the country a little closer to dealing with the sacred cow, de facto segregation, because Skelly Wright pointed out that Negro youngsters have been discriminated against in the Washington schools ever since the 1954 decision. The Court found that predominantly Negro schools had been receiving one hundred dollars less per pupil than predominantly white schools. Negro classrooms were typically overcrowded while white classrooms had more than enough space. School buildings in Negro areas were old and run-down. In addition, Negro youngsters had been relegated to the lower levels of a track system which classified its pupils on the basis of aptitude tests that were middle-class oriented.[60]

It would appear that no more evidence is needed. Extensive testing throughout the country has proven conclusively that both Negro and white students are hurt by segregated education. The highest Court of the land has consistently ruled in the twentieth century that every citizen is entitled to equal protection of the laws and that equal protection in education cannot be provided in segregated classrooms, segregated schools.

Yet, segregation persists in the schools. Eighty-seven per cent of all Negro first graders are in schools which are 50 per cent or more Negro—72 per cent in the urban North and 97 per cent in the urban South.[61]

And, what is worse, the type of education segregation is providing ghetto youth is inadequate and has failed to encourage or inspire the black student to acquire those skills needed to compete for the limited job opportunities which exist. As Kenneth Clark put it, the gross inefficiency of the black schools ". . . does the discriminating for any prejudiced employer, so that he doesn't have to do it himself."[62] Black classes are more crowded than white: in Cleveland between 1957 and 1964, 95 per cent of the units rented to relieve overcrowded classes were in nearly all-black schools; in Philadelphia in the 1965-66 school year, almost half of the black schools were overcrowded, as compared with a third of the white schools; in Chicago, the same year, 68 per cent of the mobile units were used at the nearly all-black schools, 20 per cent at the nearly all-white schools.[63] Black students are more likely to attend schools which offer no advanced courses than are their white counterparts: in a survey of metropolitan schools, it was found that 29 per cent of the Negro students were in schools with accelerated curriculums in one or more subjects, as compared with 40 per cent of the white students.[64] Library facilities are generally better in white schools—indeed, in Washington, D.C.'s, Hobson v. Hansen case, the Court found that every predominantly white school had a library, while less than 50 per cent of the predominantly black elementary schools in slum areas had libraries.[65] Ghetto and black schools are known to be in poorer physical condition. Supplies are more abundant in white schools.

Furthermore, ghetto education is not generally attuned to the realities of life. It is more than a little difficult for the ghetto child to identify with the white child portrayed in the textbook and the reader, for the picture doll is bedecked in an immaculate, unfrayed dress and is playing with expensive toys in unlittered parks.

According to Jeremy Larner, "The readers still current in practically every school are those insipid productions featuring Sally, Dick and Jane, the golden-haired cardboard tots from Sterilityville."[66] Mrs. Hattie Collins, a Hough resident, said:

> The life that is shown in "Alice and Jerry," this is for the suburb children, the beach, the playgrounds, circus, horses. We don't have anything in this book concerning inner-city children. If they didn't see the police with a horse they wouldn't know what it was and the teachers are all white and everything. . . . They are reading something opposite from their education.[67]

Perhaps the most damaging effect of the all-black school is the negative image it projects to the community at large and the students within. Teachers, incorporating the values of the society, often lower their expectations of students, and the students adjust their own aspirations accordingly. Everyone gets pulled down in the process as conceptions of self get smashed, confidence wanes, and performance is hampered.

Kenneth Clark has cited a study of ten public schools in the depressed areas of a large northern city which revealed that an "overwhelming majority" of the teachers rejected their students, finding them "inherently inferior" and therefore, "not capable of learning."[68] Since the children were deemed unteachable, the teachers didn't teach.

That teacher attitudes affect student performance was proven in an experiment performed in an elementary school in south San Francisco. Teachers were told that some of their pupils were "spurters," their potential supposedly deduced from test scores, but their names actually selected at random. After eight months the children were tested, and in fifteen out of seventeen cases, the spurters gained more IQ points than did members of the control group. The most marked gains were in the first grade where spurters achieved over fifteen more IQ points than the non-spurters in the control group.

Robert Rosenthal, the conductor of the experiment, concluded that the differential is not the result of teachers spending extra time with or on the spurters. He felt, rather, that the type of interaction between teacher and pupil—what the teacher said and how she said it—probably made the difference.[69]

Similar results were achieved in an experiment with rats at the University of North Dakota. Each student was given a group of five rats and told that they were either "maze bright" or "maze dull." Those students who believed their rats to be bright achieved better performance than those who thought their rats to be dull.

The S's [subjects] believed to be bright appeared to be learning the problem while those believed to be dull did not. These results occurred in spite of the fact that on the level of verbal report *both* groups of E's [experimenters] wanted their S's to perform well.[70]

Teachers' expectations are significant. Indeed, they are often rsponsible for determining the survival or the failure of a given child in a given school. The teacher who is convinced her class is unteachable will not teach and her class will, in fact, become unteachable.

Kenneth Clark put it another way:

Many children are now systematically categorized, classified in groups labeled slow learners, trainables, untrainables, Track A, Track B, the "Pussycats," the "Bunnies," etc. But it all adds up to the fact that they are not being taught; and not being taught, they fail.[71]

Given the circumstances, it is easy to understand the desperation of members of the black community. They are convinced that good, integrated education will never be—and they are tired of reaching for stars. The only hope they see is building quality education into their segregated schools. Along with the black power people, they are saying that since the schools are theirs, they want to control them. Mrs. Babette Edwards expresses the anger of many:

. . . my position is that no one else is educating my child and I have to see that he is educated.

I am tired of aliens sitting in a ivory tower programming my life and saying "I have the solutions to your problems." . . . We are having no more of it. If it means chaos in the entire school system, we intend to get education for our school children.[72]

Isaiah Robinson warns of where desperation may lead:

It's our kids that are being slaughtered, having no future, being dehumanized daily in this great democracy. We say "You have the democracy but we haven't seen it yet. You have the integration. We haven't seen any of it. We want justice and we are not going to get it with you. We are going to get it without you. If it brings about violence, so be it."[73]

People who talk thus are making a significant confession. They are admitting that they have no hope of achieving equality, and therefore they would make segregated education work. But, there are only so many dollars cities are willing to spend on public education. There are only so many dollars to go around. If political pressures continue to remain operative in public education as they have in the past, the people from the wealthier neighborhoods are going to continue to get at least their share of the educational dollar and probably more. Simple arithmetic will demonstrate that what is left isn't enough to rid the ghetto of its curse and its blight. Thus, deprivation will continue in black schools, regardless of who grabs and wields the power. The only way black children can get the equal education to which they are entitled is by integration. Ghettos can organize, demand and get better segregated education than they now have, but it will not equal the education provided white children. To settle for less than the best is inexcusable. By so doing, life is made too easy for the oppressors while the oppressed continue suffering.

Consequently, it is a mistake for the black power people not to concentrate more steam and pressure on achieving integration. Many of their demands will have to be met now—the white man is learning the destructive power of just a few. He knows now that it doesn't take many to set an entire section of a large city in flames. He knows the Negro does not need equal numbers to destroy the world of the majority. And he is scared. He will make concessions because he has used up all his trumps. If today's anger and emotionalism were applied to achieving integration, integration might be possible.

Yet, it is difficult to criticize anyone who is clamoring for better education for ghetto youth, whatever their means, because their concerns are shockingly real. If the country did in medicine what it does in public education, the nation's health would be in a bad way. In medicine, it siphons off its most brilliant medical scientists and presents them with the nation's toughest problems.

It puts them in technology's most modern laboratories and gives them elaborate equipment with which to work. It creates the best possible environment for them because it knows that the problems with which they have to work are the most difficult in the medical sciences. And, it rewards them by providing them the kind of environment, incentive and atmosphere which can make possible their best work, recognizing that the country's most difficult medical problems need the country's most meticulous attention.

In education, the country has actually opted to do the opposite. It knows where the most severe problems exist, yet it persists in expending its resources elsewhere—where the money is. It takes slum schools in the heart of the cities and staffs them with the most poorly prepared teachers. In some cities and towns where it is difficult to fire teachers because of tenure regulations, officials actually punish the incompetent, the wayward, by assigning them to schools in the ghetto, in the very place where youngsters need the most love, the most care, the most dedication, the most sincerity. These are the same schools that get the hand-me-down books and the out-dated materials, that have the highest overcrowding indexes, the oldest buildings, the most limited services, the schools in which the latest techniques and procedures are generally absent. It is thus that the nation compounds the problems of the poor and furthers the miseducation of ghetto youth.

It is nothing less than criminal to leave the question of schooling and the resolution of the integration issue to chance by allowing patterns of housing development to determine who goes to which school. One is hard put to explain why housing patterns should control the kind of education a child receives. If the country can conclude that people who pay more for their houses should be given a better education along with better parks and better services, then it is organizing a society which allows people to buy their way to success. It would at the same time be offering the children of those who have limited buying power a limited education, limited job training, and would thereby circumscribe their futures by limiting the job opportunities which will open to them. It would thus perpetuate most undemocratically the crippling cycle of poverty by punishing the children for their parents' poor earning power.

One can justify the perpetuation of neighborhood schools only if educational benefits accrue. And while it is easy to enumerate the administrative advantages of the neighborhood school—the convenience of parents, the convenience of students, the convenience of those who organize the boundaries—it is difficult to find anyone in the field of education who can point out even one educational benefit from the practice or the concept. If it is true that there are none, what justification can there be for their maintenance beyond administrative convenience? Is administrative convenience the goal to which we, as a nation, aspire?

5

Black Power for the Ghetto

> To create one nation has proved to be a hideously difficult task; there is certainly no need now to create two, one black and one white. But white men with far more political power than that possessed by the Nation of Islam movement have been advocating exactly this, in effect, for generations. If this sentiment is honored when it falls from the lips of Senator Byrd, then there is no reason it should not be honored when it falls from the lips of Malcom X.[1]
>
> —JAMES BALDWIN

The black ghetto has been home to millions of people for generations. And it will continue to house the country's black masses for generations to come, for even if the country's leaders change their priorities and decide to eliminate America's number one crippler, the ghetto, the ghetto residents must live somewhere while the architectural wizards plot, the social planners map strategy, construction companies bid, demolition crews raze, and builders cut ground.

It is quite likely that during such a transitional period, the Negro would remain locked in the ghetto. To whom could he turn for aid, even in an emergency situation? The white suburbs would evidence the same petty prejudices they have exhibited in the past; they will zip themselves in their ticky-tacky cloaks at the approach of any black footsteps. Within the city limits, landlords could perhaps be counted on to ship off a CARE package to Asia, but not to sacrifice a little profit to save people at home from starvation or cold. The government would undoubtedly rush through an emergency program or two, just enough to whet the appetite, but local power struggles would negate their influence and undermine their potency.

So the ghetto dweller would be left as always—a naked victim of a complex of forces which he is powerless to control, which he doesn't fully understand, and which he didn't help to create. He will again be asked to wait for a cloudless tomorrow which is just a few years of suffering away. It is true that he might feel comforted when he sees society finally moving in the right direction, and he will undoubtedly be pleased to think that his grandchildren will live to see the end of the blight of the ghetto. But, as he faces the day-to-day realities of cold pipes, wet leaks, and empty stomachs, master plans will offer little solace.

America should have learned at least one thing from its summers of riots: the black man will not sit still for any more promises to materialize, even if the promises are for the total elimination of the ghetto. The black community has learned a great deal from, or at the expense of, the white man, and the lesson it has digested quickest is that words are cheap. Wasn't it 1964 when the Civil Rights Act proclaimed that all schools were to make significant moves toward desegregation of both students and faculty? Wasn't 1967 the target year for the end of school segregation and the dual school system? Wasn't it as far back as 1868 when every American citizen was promised "equal protection under the laws"?

Yet, if the ghettos are to be eliminated, there must be a transitional period. Time must be set aside for planning, consultation, design and construction. Since white America has waited so long, since it has allowed riot conditions to develop, it must pay for its blind hypocrisy and willful neglect by making ghetto life somehow bearable in this interim, if only to keep the plans on the drafting table from going up in smoke.

THE ONLY VIABLE SOLUTION

Black power in the ghetto is the only viable solution.

Black power is the most highly charged, the most threatening term coined in this century. It has been the cadence count of hot Mississiippi marches, the rallying cry of fiery Northern riots, and the battle cry of nationwide rebellion. It has segmented American society into seething camps and challenged the basic beliefs of many Americans.

In the white world, black power has moved the frontiers of reason back a few steps; it has unleashed the blind irrationality of the bigoted. It has caused the white liberal to reexamine the core of his being.

Black power has brought out the worst in man—witness the shocking performance of the first session of the 90th Congress in the areas of civil rights and poverty. The Congress passed no civil rights legislation, no fair housing law. Indeed, President Johnson's only Civil Rights Act of 1967 was the creation of a new District of Columbia government with a Negro mayor. The Congress and the administration sabotaged their own war on poverty by weakening the Community Action Program. Under the 1964 poverty law, community action programs could reflect the voice of the people, because programs were run independently of local power structures. The Office of Economic Opportunity contracted directly with public or private nonprofit agencies to carry out the programs. The new poverty legislation has given community action programs to the local governments who can now control and make policy. The poor, as always, are about to lose what little they had.

Black power has brought out the best in man—namely, the rebirth of pride in being black. Many youngsters who are drop-outs, youngsters who are unemployed, are no longer doubting themselves because they are beginning to doubt the society that had caused them to question their own worth. Young men who would otherwise be lost, vengeful, without hope, are seeing that there are some who care enough to sacrifice for their black brother.

Because of its many connotations, because of the emotionality it inspires, black power is a term which must be defined by the one who uses it. Here, black power is intended to mean a larger voice for the Negro, greater participation and involvement of the Negro, and increased influence by the black man over his own affairs of state. As long as the ghetto dweller is powerless in his own world, that world is not his. If he is to protect and defend and not destroy the land he inhabits, that land must not be another man's birthright and the source of another man's opulence.

This is not to say that the ghetto should be completely turned over to the people who live there as that would make life too easy for the white man, for the very man who created the ghetto and intensified the problems of American blacks. White time and energy sapped the ghetto once; now those same resources must be used to help revive the life they tried to kill off. The white man still owns and controls this country and all of its resources. He can and should be used to manipulate his own system.

MANAGEMENT AND DECENTRALIZATION

The ghetto is now occupied territory. Almost everyone who has authority in it or responsibility for it is from the outside and on the outside. The system of absenteeism with its many ruthless potentates drains the ghetto of its limited resources. It drains the ghetto of its spirit, and this is the rub, for in sucking out its life, it bludgeons initiative and slaughters motivation. The President's Commission on Civil Disorders saw this point clearly when it recommended "Expanded opportunities for indigenous leadership to participate in shaping decision and policies which affect their community." More specifically, the Commissioners called for the establishment of Neighborhood Action Task Forces and neighborhood City Halls. These and similar recommendations were made with the realization that "No democratic society can long endure the existence within its major urban centers of a substantial number of citizens who feel deeply aggrieved as a group, yet lack confidence in the government to rectify perceived injustice and in their ability to bring about needed change."[2]

To revitalize the ghetto, to resuscitate its youth, ghetto residents do need to have a powerful voice in the management of ghetto affairs. To achieve such an end, decentralization of services is required. There is no doubt that regional boards in the fields of education, welfare, and housing are necessary to deal with overall policy and organization. Neighborhood groups functioning with complete autonomy would lose something in the translation of authority, namely, efficiency.

But local and neighborhood boards need to be established in addition to the regional organizations so that area inhabitants can have a voice in the services they receive and so that the services can better reflect the needs of the area. As Arthur Dunmeyer put it:

. . . unless I was living there, unless I was a part of this thing, you see I couldn't sit behind a desk and do it. I would have to know it inside and out.

I would have to get Miss Jones, who lives on the top floor who never comes downstairs, who merely sends the kids downstairs, put her in charge of upstairs. She would know more about upstairs. I wouldn't ask this other fellow, because he is the superintendent, what happens upstairs and over here. He doesn't know these things. He is the superintendent and he has his little wine concession downstairs where he sells and has parties and whatnot. He knows about this, the downstairs. I couldn't ask him about upstairs.

And I would employ each person that I did hire in any capacity, and use them to the extent of what they can offer themselves, not what the books say are right.[3]

In the field of education, for example, it is a dangerous mistake to assume that most children of the same age in all parts of a city are at the same level of development. Most scholars are now quick to admit that the problems and needs of ghetto youth are very different from those of nonghetto youngsters. Citywide curriculum is, therefore, a mistake, if not a disaster.

Uniform standards for classroom size are equally anachronistic. In the ghetto community, the ratio of teacher to student should be lower since educational deprivation in the home needs to be offset. Yet, at the behest of regional boards, ghetto ratios have generally been the same or even higher than elsewhere.

Parents organized in neighborhood groups can and should make decisions in these areas. They know well the areas of study their own children need. They can decide how best to use that portion of the educational dollar that is theirs. They can determine what the extracurricular activities of their schools should be. They can decide on the depth and breadth of counselling services. They can determine whether the school should emphasize academic training or vocational training, and, further, they can help shape the kind of vocational training their children receive. Too often, vocational education is offered in isolation and is geared to yesterday's market, especially in the ghetto, for curriculum changes and additional equipment cost money. Unrealistic training is worse than no training, for it breeds false hope and leads eventually to bitter disillusionment.

It is likely that neighborhood boards of education could accomplish what parent-teacher associations have failed to accomplish in the ghetto—the generation of interest in education on the part of parents who, for the first time, would be called upon to make important decisions. In the ghetto system, it is no oversimplification to say that most parents go to school only when summoned for disciplinary reasons; hence, they go on the defensive, wrapped in a cloud of shame. The schoolhouse quickly becomes foreign territory where parents are again called on the carpet, this time for the actions of their children.

A change in power would assuredly be accomplished by a change in attitude toward ghetto institutions. Alienation often fosters hostility. But let those who were once forbidden to "meddle" in affairs of school be asked to serve on curriculum committees, outing committees, and the like, and a positive attitude might well blossom. As the Educational Policies Commission of the National Education Association and the American Association of School Administrators stated:

> . . . It is of first importance that citizens control, within the limits of the law, the public schools, and this principle applies as much to disadvantaged citizens as to others. When people know that they have a true voice in molding the public institutions which affect their lives, they tend to work with those institutions rather than be hostile and apathetic toward them.[4]

And, from Carl Marburger, Commissioner of Education for the state of New Jersey:

> Parents who are not involved, who do not know what is taking place in the school, can certainly not reinforce what the school is doing with their children.[5]

Welfare services should similarly be decentralized. The system as it presently operates in most cities begins and ends downtown, miles from the problems, the action, and the agony. Yet downtown is for the middle class, not for the poor. The poor can't even afford the trip—it hurts the pocketbook and it hurts the pride. In Los Angeles, it takes ninety-six cents and three hours to make a round trip to the area welfare office from Watts.

Downtown officials can't feel the pulse of the ghetto. They are uninvolved and consequently often make decisions based on half-truths, distorted images. Welfare recipients are often lumped together and treated as one, when problems are as different as the individuals who arrive for assistance.

The organization of welfare services at the neighborhood level would enable neighborhood workers, indeed, recipients themselves, to man and help run welfare programs. Downtown officials working in the ghetto would gain understanding which cannot be transmitted over long-distance wires. By beginning to look at the poor in their own habitat, they might well begin to understand the culture of the poor, the strengths of the culture of the poor. Downtown workers might begin to realize that they can't see the ghetto through middle-class lenses nor can they sit in judgment on cold middle-class benches. As Claude Brown pointed out, two worlds mean two value systems:

> . . . in the Negro ghettos throughout the country, these things that are considered criminal by society, the solid citizen, aren't considered criminal. It is like a war between them and us, the society which oppresses us, and us, the oppressed. When a guy goes to jail, it is O.K. You are looked up to, if you are a successful hustler, you have a big Cadillac and you have always got $300 in your pocket, you are taking numbers, you are selling drugs, you are a stickup artist, you are anything, you are a prostitute, anything you may be doing, you are a con man, a hustler . . . You learn these games at certain ages. . . . As long as you were making it, as long as you were a success, that is why in Harlem people respect the guy who is always clean.
>
> You know, he has on a $200 silk suit every day, $55 alligator shoes and this sort of thing. He drives a big Cadillac, and, they know he is winning the war. He is a soldier, he is a real soldier. He is a general in the community. If he gets busted, well, he is just a prisoner of war.[6]

Illegitimacy, for example, is a fact of life. Middle-class moralizing won't make it disappear and abortions are not part of the ghetto system. Ghetto residents, welfare recipients, probably have a lot to say about illegitimacy and should be given the chance to teach and administer programs to deal with the problem. They start with a great advantage—knowledge of the problem as it is. They are not blinded by bursts of self-righteous indignation.

Even in the area of recreational services and programs, the ghetto has had no voice. Have ghetto youngsters ever been asked what kind of recreation programs they want? Have ghetto youth ever been asked to help decide what schedules should be? Have programs ever been planned around job schedules or has officialdom been so interested in uniformity of playground hours that ghetto playground programs are underattended because the youths are working?

No one should be surprised when ghetto youth, schooled in the ways of the street, men before their time, rebel against recreation programs which are strictly regimented, overplanned, the boxing-at-ten-football-at-eleven syndrome. Rigidity in play isn't part of the culture.

Health services ought to be where the people are. Ghetto communities generally house more children per square acre; hence, they should house more health facilities per square mile. Neighborhood units ought to be functioning around the clock, not just weekdays from nine to five when most people are working. Officials often state that this is impossible, since nurses won't go into the ghetto at night. That may be, but why not train area residents to do the work?

One of the great medical problems in the Negro ghetto community is that of prenatal care. Middle-class people take for granted that when a woman becomes pregnant, she will see a doctor. In the ghetto, pregnancy is often diagnosed by the patient and treated by the patient. Most reason that since they are not ill, they need not seek assistance. Barring complications, they go to a doctor only at the time of delivery. For this reason alone, the rate of Negro youngsters who die in stillbirth is amazingly high. Figures based primarily in D.C. General and Freedmen's Hospital, the Washington hospitals servicing most of the city's poor blacks, indicate that in 1964 the infant mortality rate was 34.7 per 1000 births. Until 1966, half of the women delivering at D.C. General had had no prenatal care. The figure is about one-third now.[7] In 1963, in all of New York City, there were 25.9 infant deaths per 1,000 birth; in Bedford Stuyvesant there were 37.0, in Central Harlem, 38.1 and in East Harlem, 39.1.[8]

If ghetto women were to work in clinics, they would quickly learn the value of prenatal care. Their discoveries would be shared with neighbors and friends and perhaps the number of stillbirths would be significantly decreased.

EMPLOYMENT

The opening up of a new job market in the ghetto to the ghetto black would be an important outgrowth of the decentralization of services. The stress on *new* is all-important here, for blacks are tired of the dead-end jobs which require little intelligence, the jobs which are strictly menial—the very jobs which are open to the ghetto dweller now. Decentralization could open up a wide array of respectable, challenging jobs, jobs which the ghetto resident would feel proud to hold.

Many have argued over the past five to ten years that America would be wise to create more jobs for the poor. They have pleaded with industry and government to hire the unemployed and teach them new skills. They have urged Federal legislation that would reach even the hard-core unemployed. Climaxing many such efforts, President Johnson, in his 1968 State of the Union address, called on industry to create 500,000 jobs within three years for the hard-core unemployed.

While all such measures are needed, while their enactment represents a step forward, they still smack somewhat of paternalism. They are unduly condescending, for the poor black is still reduced to accepting something—this time a job—that the white man decides to give when the white man decides to give it. He is offered a job not because of his talents or his skills, but in spite of them, because the nation has decided to decrease its unemployment figures.

Contrast this to the situation which would arise were the new ghetto jobs created. In the ghetto, the nonprofessional resident has special talents and highly specialized skills. He has firsthand knowledge of his community. He is poor and black, like others in the ghetto, and he knows what it feels like to be poor and black. He comes by his knowledge and his feelings naturally—he doesn't need to rely on books, statistics or weekend strolls to sop up local color.

He has some savvy, some know-how. Outsiders may know how to get at some of the problems from the top, but he knows how to get at them from the bottom. He can work from the inside, where it counts for his people. He's probably been on welfare, so he knows the system's inadequacies; he's lived in the ghetto school, so he knows its teachings.

The ghetto resident knows the people in his neighborhood. He is familiar with the numbers runners, the alcoholics, the pushers, the delinquent youngsters. He knows something about how they operate and why they succeed.

Finally, and most important, he can communicate in the ghetto world. His probings are not likely to elicit "No, sir-yes, sir" salutes. He isn't under immediate attack, suspected because he is another color or because he speaks in high-class phrases and wears alien garb.

Indigenous workers in the ghetto, therefore, come to the ghetto labor market with a special kind of expertise. Their diplomas were earned from living and suffering in the city's cellars. That they do not hold a traditional diploma means only that they did not learn the traditional course, the course *outside life*. But their special knowledge makes them special in the ghetto; they are privy to something that the white-skinned Ph.D. social worker is not. And they must be employed—in large numbers—for only they can inspire ghetto youth.

There are many jobs that are needed and that can be created in the ghetto for the ghetto. Almost every service provided in the city's slums is inadequate, from the educational enterprise to the recreational program. In just about every area, there is an insufficient number of professionals to even begin to deal with the problems. There is no service area that could not benefit from the use of aides. In every area, there are services that trained professionals now render which people without training could perform adequately. Indeed, in every area, there are services which "outside" professionals are called upon to perform which most are incapable of performing because of their middle-class orientation. Professionals need be free for professional work—they must also be guided in the ways of the poor. Alone the outside professional cannot help but shortchange the ghetto resident; with the ghetto's help, he can begin to make up for the past.

In the field of education, teachers often spend more time behind paper than they do in front of students. This is undoubtedly one of the greatest tragedies of American education. It is pathetically ironic that such a situation exists in cities which have an overflowing reservoir of labor.

Many of the tasks that teachers perform don't require a degree in education. Marking certain examinations, keeping attendance records, filling out report cards, monitoring study halls, monitoring cafeterias, running and caring for audio-visual equipment, are but a few. Teacher assistants are the obvious solution and they are beginning to be used, but interestingly enough, most of them are expected to have college or high school diplomas.

There are many residents of the ghetto, male and female, parents and unmarrieds, who are degree-less, but who should and could be working right in the classroom. The high school dropout should be hired and given just enough training to make him useful as an aide. He need not be put through the whole school curriculum. He probably wouldn't make it. But he might stick to the program were he allowed to study in high school in the morning, and then to work afternoons in elementary and junior high schools. Other work-study programs have been highly successful. It is likely that such a work-study arrangement would lessen the dropout problem, lighten the teacher load, and help the student in many ways, not the least of which would be through placing men in the schools.

Men with college training generally don't find their way to elementary school teaching. The consequence is that middle-class females are running the country's elementary schools. In the ghetto, the matriarchal household is thereby paralleled by the matriarchal classroom and school to the detriment of the students. The boys work under a double handicap—the teacher not only represents another value system, but also another sex. What chance is there for real communication?

Neighborhood people can serve well as counseling aides. They could provide a badly needed link between the home and the school. They could help the guidance counselor from the other side of the tracks get her bearings, learn a new set of signals, the new language.

In *New Careers for the Poor,* Arthur Pearl and Frank Riessman suggest that five teacher functions—aide, assistant, associate, teacher, supervising teacher—should exist along a continuum and that advancement from position of entry to the professional level "be negotiable on the basis of talent and motivation." They suggest that the position of teacher aide be open to all, regardless of years in school or record. The aide would require little training and if successful, would be encouraged to continue his education. His duties would range from supervising recess and lunch to assisting students with special projects. An assistant would need two years of college and would help prepare classroom material, correct papers and assist students at home. The associate, with four years of college, would perform the same duties as the professional, but would be under supervision.[9]

The greatest value in the Pearl-Riessman proposal lies in the upward mobility available to even the untrained aide. Workers, with the school's encouragement and help, are asked to continue their studies while working and are invited to move up the ladder.

Coupled with the fact that police departments need more power is the fact that police-community relations are strained to the point of breaking. Most racial riots have been sparked by a police incident. Ghetto residents now regard the police as an occupying army, not wanted, imposed by other powers stronger than they. They feel the same antagonism toward the blue-costumed white man that the French, the Poles, the Yugoslavs, the Czechs felt toward the Germans during the Occupation. The police, after all, like the Germans, are from another land—enemy territory. In Washington, D.C., in September 1966, only 18.6 per cent of the members of the Metropolitan Police Department were Negroes—this when Negroes comprised 63 per cent of the population.[10] The invaders speak a different language, represent a foreign culture. They appear to have unlimited and unchallenged power and often use it mercilessly. They take advantage of women; their very presence mocks and emasculates men.

The only way to lessen the antagonism and relax a tense community is for police departments to hire ghetto residents to serve in ghetto areas. What a simple solution, for all it takes is the creation of a different type of qualifying examination. To date, the system has made its judgments on the basis of education, giving much weight to such seemingly irrelevant qualities as verbal skill in traditional English.

Testing experts would do well to devise an examination which could measure such intangibles as sensitivity to the ghetto community, the ability to identify with and relate to the ghetto resident, the ability to speak to and understand the person one will be paid to protect. A man does not necessarily need to be a college graduate or even a high school graduate to be an effective policeman. It is not the quality of his education, but the quality of his understanding, the quality of his soul, which counts.

The police department has, for too long, been the refuge of the weak who covet the power and the authority of the badge. It is time for those who seek justice to get a chance.

Resentment of lawmen in the ghetto will undoubtedly increase if police departments continue to recruit outside the ghetto, if they continue to push for new programs like those which attempt to draw men into the force from the armed services. Bringing people back from killing in wars and putting them on ghetto streets can't help but have an explosive psychological effect in the slums. It isn't possible to scare an oppressed people into submission; attempting to do so will only cause festering hatreds to surface.

By recruiting outside the ghetto, the police department tells the ghetto resident he is not qualified to police himself. He is not able to accept responsibility for his own acts or misacts. Someone else must. And so the ghetto dweller is indirectly encouraged to work at another level, against the law; if he is not good enough to work *in* it, why should he work *with* it?

The President's Commission on Law Enforcement and Administration of Justice recommended that police departments have three types of officers—the community service officer, the police officer, and the police agent. The community service officer would serve in an aide capacity. Uniformed but unarmed, he would work with the youth on his beat. The Commission suggests that this officer should be under twenty-one and need not meet the standard educational requirements of the force. He could even have a minor offense record. Under the department's sponsorship, he could get good training on the force and could continue his studies in order to move up to a higher office. Such programs would give ghetto youth a chance, would bring the department closer to the community.[11]

A program that worked successfully in Washington, D.C., in the hot 1967 summer was Project ALERT, a program which hired twenty-three young ghetto men, ages nineteen to twenty-six, to help avert flare-ups in seven of Washington's tense precincts. The youths typified ghetto residents in their dislike and distrust of authority, their alienation from the white power structure and their lack of confidence in the police.

The youths walked into potentially dangerous situations, gave citizens a chance to air their grievances and offered alternatives to violence as a solution. Since they were known in their neighborhoods, their advice was often heeded. They didn't have to deal with the rank suspicion and distrust the alien faces.

In addition to making police forces more representative, police-community relations programs are needed, and community people must do the community relations half of the job, not the police. It matters not how bad their grammar, how limited their education. If the goal is truly increasing communication and bettering relations, area residents are the only people to work with the community. They have the broad, deep contacts needed—they are not loathed for what they represent.

In the area of welfare, investigators should be hired right out of the ghetto, indeed from the welfare rolls. In addition to increasing employment, such a strategy would undoubtedly yield a higher degree of cooperation between recipient and worker because a different type of investigatory service would be provided. Wherever welfare clients have organized, they have organized against the night riders, the night snoopers who peek under beds, who knock on the door Sunday morning to check and see if someone is hiding, to check and see whether there really is no man in the house. The whole ghetto community is repulsed by the inhumanity and lack of privacy afforded them, so they organize against a system which they feel takes advantage of them because they are poor. If they were the welfare investigators, other methods would probably be found that would not be so repulsive, so dehumanizing.

There are many other kinds of jobs in welfare which neighborhood workers could administer: they could dispense relief, take and file welfare applications, or serve as intake workers. No special training is needed to do this work. It is easy enough to teach people to take applications, to hand out food or food stamps.

Hospitals could make use of ghetto residents as technicians' aides, nurses' aides, and orderlies. Ghetto subprofessionals could do intake work, serve as receptionists, ward clerks or practical nurses.

In the field of recreation, it makes no sense to require a college degree of the man who runs the playground. Athletic ability and love of children are the only two reasonable prerequisites. Yet, the ghetto teenager who wants to be a playground supervisor and who won't be accepted in another job downtown, time and time again, loses out to the button-down chap with the diploma who could easily find work elsewhere.

Public safety departments could use aides to keep the firehouses in order, to paint and polish equipment. Ghetto residents could be employed to inspect their own parking meters, to give tickets for illegal parking.

Social work agencies could hire ghetto women to serve as visiting homemakers. In this capacity they could visit public housing and other low-income families and offer practical advice in budgeting, sewing, cleaning, childcare, cooking and shopping. Health departments could hire ghetto women to make similar visits to offer advice about free innoculations, prenatal services, and infancy care.

It is unfair and grossly inaccurate to assume that an increase in jobs and changes in job standards are equivalent to a lowering of these standards. In selecting policemen, for example, if New York City were to require its cops on ghetto beats to have knowledge of the ghetto, its language and its customs, instead of a high school diploma, the argument could be made that it would be thereby raising the standards. The policemen selected might well be less versed in academic subjects, but they would undoubtedly be better trained in an area more relevant to their work—the protection of the ghetto dweller.

Secondly, it is possible actually to lower standards, academic and otherwise, without impairing the quality of service to be rendered. Sometimes, the mere act of lowering standards is accompanied by better performance because the job recipients are so glad to be given a challenging opportunity, a chance at life, that they work as hard as possible to produce and to prove their worth.

There are many jobs which today require college degrees which ought to be examined to see if an advanced degree is really necessary. If not, society's best interest would be served if the employer would reject the college graduate in favor of the qualified ghetto resident. This, not because the poor have a monopoly on sensitivity, but because college graduates can go elsewhere with their wares and doors will not automatically close.

Also, it is only right that preferential attention be shown the black ghetto dweller. The black man has been participating in a race with the white man for three hundred years in America. But the black man has been running with his arms tied, his legs bound, his eyes blindfolded, while the white man has been running free. It is, therefore, inaccurate to assume that opportunity will be equalized today merely by removal of the bindings and the blindfold. There is no way that the black man can catch up even if he *is* put at the starting line with his white counterpart. He was outdistanced a long time ago. The most he can hope to do is enjoy his equal opportunity and keep the gap from widening; if he is very lucky, he might close it a little. Closing the gap completely is a physical and mental impossibility, unless the man he is racing falls flat on his face. And that won't happen unless the country first falls apart. In order to lessen the black man's handicap, the country must be willing to give him special attention. Preferential treatment must be his in the job market.

A SHARE IN THE PROFITS

There can be no black power without some profit sharing. The average black citizen is basically a wage earner, living from payday to payday, and not very well. There is no way for the black man in America to catch up by remaining a wage earner. At best, he can manage to close the gap a little bit. But if the Negro is ever really going to catch up, he must be given his forty acres and a mule. If he is ever really going to get out of the wage-earner class, he is going to have to have some help from his country. The poverty program is a start, but it is handicapped because it provides services instead of providing the opportunity for the poor to develop some economic security. OEO, although it is the best we have, has allowed the middle-class to appropriate for itself the best jobs, leaving the poor the crumbs to fight over.

More meaningful would be the underwriting by government and private industry of ghetto-based, ghetto-run, ghetto-controlled cooperatives. Negroes could own and run laundry and dry-cleaning establishments, cooperative bakeries, shoe shops, garages, catering industries, day-care centers. Pride, Inc., in Washington, D.C., is attempting to move in this direction. Pride, as stated above, was conceived during the heated summer of 1967 by black men and boys and financed by a grant by the United States Department of Labor. It originally was in business to clean dirt from alleys and kill rats left over by the Sanitation Department. The young men now intend to create and run their own cooperatives, and a two-million-dollar grant from the Federal government will allow them to get started. Once they begin, they will develop contracts with business and the District government and will seek autonomy.

Pride men are representative ghetto youths—most of them are dropouts, some are potential bomb throwers. One young man, now a supervisor, was about to resort to theft in order to feed his family when Pride came along. The man, a high school dropout with a record, had been unable to find work. He finally managed to get enrolled in a work-training program which paid a monthly allowance and which got his family into a low-income project. "Awakened one night by a rat running across his chest, he jumped out of bed to find another in his three-month-old baby's crib. . . . Looking for decent housing, he was dropped from the training program after missing several sessions." He was about "to get money any way he could."[12]

Pride has given many a new lease on life. The establishment of a network of cooperatives will give each member something of his own, something to fight for. The business each helps to run will be his business. He will be concerned with profit and loss—his profit and loss, not someone else's. Consequently, interest and enthusiasm for the project are high. Every participant wants to work hard to make it work.

In the area of housing under Section 221(d)(3) of the National Housing Act of 1961, churches and other charitable organizations are given a means to finance housing for low- to middle-income people. FHA is empowered to insure mortgages on new or rehabilitated rental and cooperative housing below the market interest rate. Thus, without any down payment, a nonprofit organization can develop a business which it will own in forty years. Since no profit is to be made, the rents are low enough not to work a hardship on the building's tenants, although they are high enough to pay off the debt and also to provide good maintenance service. Churches can undertake such housing co-ops for their own membership.

The Model Inner City Community Organization will carry this idea one step further. MICCO plans to develop the machinery that will enable people to obtain the kind of low-cost housing that they need. It also wants to train people in the neighborhood to do the kinds of jobs that will be necessary. In other words, it hopes to train the ghetto's young men to be the carpenters, the electricians, and the plumbers who will serve the community. Such an idea, although anathema to organized labor, would guarantee that urban renewal would not be used as an exploitative tool to take away the property and the profit from the community.

That black men in the ghetto can run businesses successfully is not even a matter for conjecture. Black men have for years run most of the white business establishments in the ghetto. In some ghetto businesses, the owner is seen only when it is time to collect the bills; the landlord is seen only when the rent is due. Negroes make the purchases, run the stores, man the machinery, deliver the goods. They even keep the records. The only thing they don't share is the profit.

The establishment of cooperatives would stop the money, the capital, the manhood from gushing out of the ghetto. Today, the dollars that come into Harlem and Watts on Friday night are, by Monday, in the fat, white pockets of merchants, rent collectors and creditors. The ghetto is once again left barren and stripped of all that spells incentive and hope.

EQUAL OPPORTUNITY VERSUS EQUAL RESULTS

Since strengthening the ghetto can only be an interim measure, black power is needed not to lock people in or to help people adjust to their chains, but rather to help the ghetto dweller burst forth and out into a world free of all encumbrances. Equal opportunity is, therefore, not enough. The aim is equal results, and equal results cannot be achieved by putting ill-matched opponents behind the same starting line.

America long ago accepted the fact that the veteran is entitled to a preference in the federal job market. The country reasoned that while serving in the armed forces men lose ground on the civilian front and should thereby be given special treatment, a chance to catch up upon discharge. Thus, today, whenever a veteran takes an examination, he gets an additional ten points added to his final score, even if he was out of circulation for only two or three years.

If equal results are to be obtained, the black man must be given at least the same ten-point preference as the veteran, not only in employment tests but in the housing market and in the educational field.

The price tag for sobriety, for peace in the ghetto in the transition years, is the best teachers, smaller classes, more industry and more jobs—a chance for a fair deal. The price is preferential treatment. If the costs are financially or psychologically unacceptable, America will have other costs to reckon with and may someday wish that all it had to do was pay a tab. When men begin to fall in white backyards, even A. Philip Randolph's $185,000,000,000 Freedom Budget will seem a pittance.

6

Elimination of the Ghetto

> This, then, is the end of his striving; to be a co-worker in the kingdom of culture, to escape both death and isolation, to husband and use his best powers and his latent genius.[1]
>
> —W. E. B. DuBois

We have seen that the Negro's heritage in America at best has been one of willful neglect at the behest of his white brother. At worst, it has been conscious subjugation by a white community which has stripped him of his manhood, his pride and his incentive by throwing him into the pit of the city and daring, indeed taunting, him to survive amidst squalor, disease, unemployment, depravity. What little the black man has left when he enters the city's bowels, the ghetto kills off forever.

Everything, that is, but vengeance. For the street-corner textbooks of the inner city teach the lessons of hatred well, even to the student who refuses to listen. The depravity, the ugliness, the powerlessness, all combine to make learning easy. Classes are short—men graduate early.

For years, the ghetto's hatred turned in on itself. Blacks victimized blacks, acting out street-corner dramas in uncontrolled rage, convulsed by spasms of self-hatred and masochistic feelings, lashing out at innocent brothers for the sake of conquering someone—anyone—to prove that one's existence somehow mattered.

But with Watts and its three-year fiery aftermath, the hatred changed its complexion. It threatened black and white alike, the ghetto dwelling and the palatial estate, and so brought hope in the ashes. For, if it were only to the advantage of the Negro to eliminate the ghetto, the task would be an impossibility, power structures being what they are. For over fifty-six years America's Negro ghettos have grown in number and in intensity to the concern of a mere handful. For over fifty-six years the inner city has choked while America's leaders looked on in relative silence. It is true that in 1965 some middle-class consciences were stirred when Kenneth Clark published *Dark Ghetto*. But it is equally true that the moving account was quickly forgotten by the unknowing and uncaring who make the decisions which matter.

Watts hit home as no book could, even though it told the same tale of desperation. Watts and Detroit and Newark cut into the white man's profit and threatened to eat their way into his secure, manicured world. Consequently, fear mounted, concern was evidenced and stopgap programs were rushed through legislatures and administrative agencies to help the downtrodden. Goaded on by scared politicians, highest-level bureaucrats, who generally don't concern themselves with deciding what programs are to be funded and why, set aside millions of dollars to improve ghetto conditions. Administrators cut through skeins of governmental red tape to rush first aid into riot-torn cities.

When the summer of 1967 ended, Watts seemed a bonfire. The white man was left perplexed, apprehensive, scarred, in prayer. But he, too, had learned a lesson from the street corner: no longer was the ghetto only the Negro's problem, if only because its destructive fury could no longer be contained.

Indeed, it is only because the destructiveness of the ghetto threatens to tear down ghetto walls and spew its fury forth into the white world that America is showing so much concern over the plight of its cities today. It lives in fear of next summer and the next while it searches for easy answers, instant panaceas which will make the problem disappear and avert further hurt.

So far the best white America's enlightened leaders have come up with are programs to increase employment and job training. Such programs are, unfortunately, mere palliatives. No one would deny their value—they do give a person a chance at life. While waiting for the surgeon to cut out the cancer, it is necessary to convince the patient that surgery is needed, to keep the patient alive so that he can benefit from surgery, to enable him to function as well as possible in the meantime. Yet nothing short of surgery—eliminating the ghetto—will ultimately save, for nothing else will quiet the cries, lessen the anger, weaken the demands of the ghetto dweller, for he knows he has a new-found power. He is moved by a relentless drive fed on hate, and he has nothing to lose, for he has nothing.

America has to understand that it must act at once. Its alternatives are limited, and time has indeed run out. If it is to rid itself of the problems of the ghetto forever, if its cities are to survive, America must eliminate the ghetto and the ghetto mentality. Three approaches are needed: opening up the society so that the Negro will have a full, participating voice at all levels; opening up the society so that the Negro has a full stake in it; and redistributing the population to make the first two approaches possible.

PARTICIPATION AT ALL LEVELS

This nation must open itself up so that the full and equal voice of the Negro will be heard. The black American must be permitted to participate in American affairs, not just in Negro affairs. It is indisputable that today the Negro voice is heard only on those issues which directly affect the black man, and even then, it is often tuned out. Witness Governor Rockefeller's conference on public welfare which was held at the beginning of November 1967 to celebrate the one-hundredth anniversary of welfare in New York. Of approximately one hundred fifty participants, there were two Negroes. No welfare recipients were present.

One need not look very far to find evidence that even the most educated whites often change the frequency when the Negro voice is heard. A university in the Washington, D.C. area planned a couple of seminars in the winter of 1967 on the problems of American cities. The consultant list of about ten names contained not a single Negro. It is hardly conceivable that a university in the heart of America's most heavily populated Negro city could plan a seminar of this type for leadership personnel with an all-white consultant roster with the riots still reverberating, with Washington loaded with Negroes who are competent and well trained in urban affairs. How could a university be so insensitive to the very issues it wanted to probe? How meaningful could such talks be?

Most whites are still imbued with the desire to do things *for* Negroes. They find it difficult to change their paternalistic stance. They remain immobile in a time of change and upheaval, steadfast in their "we-can-solve-their-problem-for-them" creed.

The universities, in many ways, are as far away from the recognition that Negroes need solve many of their own problems as is business. The ivory tower is still encloaked; the cries from the cities have not yet penetrated the academic curtain. And this seems tragic, because in a seat of learning the ingredients of change and the process of change ought to be understood. The intellectual community should be vocal in proving to the nation that experimentation cannot be performed if the material that need be tested is absent. Substitutes won't do, regardless of the quality of the expert who is doing the probing.

White political leaders, too, should be in the vanguard, but they have for too long reflected the lowest level of ignorance of their constituents. Instead of attempting to raise the level of understanding in their areas of responsibility, the typical Congressman or Senator tries to mirror the majority opinion, however damaging or corrupting it may be.

When Senator Eastland was verbally attacked as an obstructionist at a Washington, D.C., meeting, someone rose to his defense and claimed that the Senator was really in favor of integrating Mississippi football teams. Is this leadership? Should a Senator be judged by his private, unpublicized beliefs or by his public actions? For Senator Eastland, with all his power in Mississippi and in the Senate, to believe in integrated sports is not enough. It is only as he uses his power to wield change that his beliefs matter. The man who votes against legislation to promote equal opportunity cannot get away with claiming he's really for it, by claiming he must voice opposition to please the people back home. Leadership is supposed to lead—not follow. The nation is in trouble now precisely because it is led from the rear, because leaders at all levels suffer from a failure of nerve. The believer in equal opportunity must vote *for* such legislation and then convince the people back home that he did the right thing.

There has been relatively little concern shown by most whites for the plight of the Negro in America. Yet when plans to deal with the Negroes' problems have been on the drawing board, white America has been so anxious to draw up the blueprints that it has convinced itself that the Negro is incapable of planning for himself. Mrs. Carole King, a member of an organization of Cleveland welfare mothers, testified before the U.S. Commission on Civil Rights that she had suggested to welfare officials "that we all get together with county, State and Federal officials to sit down and discuss the problems." They felt it was a ". . . ridiculous offer. . . . They would probably be surprised. We probably could work something out that would actually help the mothers and fathers that are on the welfare programs. We are not even accepted as human beings. . . ."[2]

One way the Negro can get a participating voice through his own efforts is through the full and intelligent use of politics. If Negroes are elected to high offices, the Negro voice will come through, his needs will begin to be satisfied. It is true that Negroes can become tools of the system just as white politicians do, yet the Negro presumably brings more sensitivity to the job.

Carl Stokes, in his primary campaign for Cleveland's mayoralty, used the slogan, "DON'T VOTE FOR A NEGRO, vote for a man." The slogan was bothersome to many Negroes. Many found it offensive. "Don't vote JUST for a Negro, vote for a man" would have sat better with these people because they think it all right to vote for a man because he is black. And, indeed, preferential consideration is in order when the mandate reads "Undo three hundred years of discrimination." Black men must vote for black men because they are black. This is one reason the Negro community mobilized behind Carl Stokes. His blackness was part of his appeal. His staunch supporters didn't knock themselves out campaigning solely because he is a good politician or a nice guy. Martin Luther King, Jr., the Urban League and other organizations didn't form a coalition to support Stokes only because they liked him. They discriminated in his favor because he is Negro primarily, and therefore representative of them, and also because he is bright, competent, and qualified and has a right to Cleveland's mayoralty.

Many businessmen supported Stokes because they knew he was qualified and because they knew that a vote for him was a vote for time. Cleveland's major problem in 1967 was the struggle between blacks and whites and the polarization that was taking place because of that struggle. Businessmen realized that Stokes, being black, could neutralize the situation to some degree, at least for a while.

But the business elite need also realize that bestowing upon a Negro the title of Mayor means little. What counts is the power and influence of the office. If the business community covets the power and the influence, it will relegate its Mayor to a figurehead status and make him incapable of delivering. Stokes will thereby be in trouble and Cleveland will experience greater difficulty than ever before.

Negroes ought to be in leadership roles of government especially when the principal problem of the day is violence in the cities. Who understands as well the problems of the ghetto? Who knows better what deprivation does to a man? Negro-white relationships are the crux of our urban problems. The white side has been heard from, the results belie any understanding, insight, compassion or intelligence. The game won't be lost if the ball is shared with the other team.

This is not to say that Negroes should not actively support sympathetic white politicians. It is an oversimplification, and fallacious, to assume that white politicians, by virtue of their color, are not concerned or fair. It is equally untrue, on the other hand, to think that whites can fully understand the problems the Negro faces. Therefore, the Negro voter is left with the responsibility of sensitizing white politicians and of then showing loyalty to those who become sensitized. He should also make demands when his candidate is triumphant in return for the support offered.

Another route to full Negro participation is their presence on appointive boards and commissions at the Federal, State and local levels. Unfortunately, this route is marked out in large part by whites, for whites still make most major decisions and appointments.

The Board of Education in Washington, D.C., is appointed pursuant to a quota system. For fifty years, until 1962, the black quota was three out of nine seats. In 1962, the quota was upped to four, one less than a majority. This, in a city with a population that is over 60 per cent black, a school population that is more than 90 per cent black.

Under the old district government in Washington, D.C., there were ninety-one boards and commissions which dealt with all aspects of district affairs, from the Advisory Council to the Commissioners to the issuance of hackers' licenses. At the inception of its Leadership Development Program in 1964, the Washington Urban League found that Negroes were represented on less than half of these boards and commissions; when they were, it was in large measure only token representation.

All too often the white man justifies his prejudiced decision to make commissions all white by claiming that there are no qualified Negroes to serve. This is the same mentality which keeps offices and factories and college classrooms lily-white. If qualifications were compared, whites on commissions would probably be found to surpass their Negro counterparts—but only in accumulated wealth and in accumulated college and advanced degrees, not in knowledge of the problems under study or in the duties which must be performed. If one studies the decisions of the various commissions appointed in recent years, one will find that white voices generally call for increased services. Basically, whites accept the system, with its inequities and shortcomings, and focus on how to relieve the problem—how to provide more food and jobs without rooting out the causes of starvation and unemployment. The best white men, those who understand the issues, rarely think in terms of what creates the problems. But the Negro who is in touch with his people is mainly preoccupied with activities of prevention. He wants to change the system which has created the problems.

The entire communications media must be revamped, or certainly refocused, if the Negro is to be seen for what he is and heard as he speaks. The communications industry has done more to create and promote a negative image of the Negro than any other single group or industry in American society. Stereotypes and myths are the order of the day; the Negro is rarely seen as an individual, but usually as a group.

Ted Poston, a newspaperman writes:

The majority of the Southern editors and publishers have been cynically defending a myth that they know to be untrue—white superiority, Negro indolence, and a baseless contention that the region's magnolia-scented values would triumph over the moral and legal might of the federal government.

At the same time, during my thirty-five years in this business, I have observed Northern editors and publishers creating and perpetuating a subtler myth: that Northern Negroes really are a monolithic mass, not plain individual Americans, and that they must be viewed and reported in that context.[3]

Is this the reason that a survey of American whites taken nationally in 1963 revealed that 68 per cent believe that Negroes "laugh a lot," 66 per cent believe Negroes have no ambition, 60 per cent believe they "smell different," 55 per cent believe they "have looser morals," 46 per cent think their homes aren't neat, and a full 41 per cent believe they "want to live off the handout"?[4] News coverage must be at least part of the reason.

William B. Monroe, Jr., states that ". . . the white people of this country should be introduced to the Negroes who are not on the street demonstrating . . . Whites, North and South, rarely see . . . Negroes as people, decent, hard-working, attractive, human."[5]

The mass media all too often state or imply that there are so many opportunities available to the Negro, if he would only take advantage. The Federal Aviation Administration, for example, produced the film "How About Billy Wilson?" that was meant to be a youth incentive piece for Negro youth. Jackie Robinson narrated. The film showed an integrated group of students going to the airport where they were given a guided tour. In the airport scenes, there were hardly any Negroes performing the jobs shown. The narration seemed to suggest, "Here are opportunities that Negroes are not using and so we're showing you these opportunities." Yet, throughout the film there was no recognition or acknowledgement of the fact that part of the reason Negroes haven't been employed is because of discrimination.

If Negro youths are to gain the self-confidence needed to seek, obtain and retain good jobs, they need to understand the realities. They need to understand that black men are not behind ticket counters, not because they can't do the job, but because they weren't wanted until recently and because now they are wanted only in token number. Films and news clippings can't leave this fact for youths to deduce themselves.

The media must assist the Negro to understand that he had a noble and glorious past and that black men have made many contributions to American society and culture that have gone unrecorded due to the wishes of racist whites who wanted to damn the entire Negro race. The Negro youth should be shown time and again that Negroes before him have been involved in American life and that all Negroes are not parasites living off the fat of the land that someone else created and built.

And, as the Riot Commission has recommended, the media must assist the white man to understand what it means to live in the black ghetto. Whites must be shown the helplessness and the never-ceasing frustration of being black in a land that honors only the white. The media must introduce and familiarize whites with Negro history, Negro culture, Negro art, Negro music.

The frustrations manifested by Negroes' problems get considerably more attention than the problems themselves. The frustrations reflect upon the group rather than upon the condition. The media refuse to talk about racial discrimination. Rather, they talk about actions taken by Negroes because of racial discrimination and therefore never deal with the problem itself. What is not easily visible gets by-passed. "A riot in Los Angeles and a sit-in in North Carolina are fine subjects for visual treatment. But what about an exploration of the dual system of justice in the South or the problems of Negro employment in the North?"[6]

More recently, the press is guilty of creating leaders for and of Negroes. In granting first-page coverage to that black militant who dares speak out strongly and irreverently against the Establishment, the press tells the public that he is newsworthy; and if he is worthy of so much space, so much attention, society reasons he must be powerful. Thus, do many newspapers give "respectability" to irresponsibility, an act which Ted Posten feels to be ". . . the greatest crime of many of our Northern papers in these times of national stress."[7]

Finally, the voice of the Negro will be heard only if the Negro delegation can stop going downtown—if downtown begins appearing in the ghetto. The ghetto is where the sounds are; it is where the smells and the action are. City Hall can't learn in isolation. It can't feel with the hands of others. The black man knows the white man's world, but the white man is ignorant of all that is black. On a stifling Monday night in the summer of 1967, a riot in Washington was near. At the urging of the Washington Urban League, eighty-five community and business leaders decided to hold a meeting to discuss the situation with the Negro community leaders. The whites, in predictable fashion, proposed convening the session in City Hall's air-conditioned conference room. The Negro leaders insisted upon holding the meeting where the problem was so that Whitey might this one time get the feel, the smell, and heat of it. Everyone suffered that night, but none so intensely as the white man. For not only did he swelter, he also learned fear—he was in black hands for four hours; he was not calling the signals. He had to sit and listen while militant leaders cursed him and damned him for his shortsightedness, his apathy. But that wasn't the worst of it, for those sharing the church with him, despite their animosity, were willing to talk and work with him. There were others who refused. They walked outside the church, their chants haunting the whites within, because they called for an end to all negotiations between black and white. This was war, and the white man was behind enemy lines.

On the white side of the line, no one knew war had been declared. Those who witnessed the skirmish went back to report, but all too many still refused to listen and believe. That is why white men must go into the ghetto themselves. Secondhand reports lose too much of their impact in the translation.

A FULL STAKE IN AMERICAN SOCIETY

The Negro wants a full stake in American society. He wants to own some of this country. He has to share its wealth. For even a full voice without a stake is a voice that will eventually die out. Were the wealth that the Negro controlled in America in proportion to his population, racial problems would be less weighty. The middle- and upper-income blacks have a small stake in this country which they seek to build and protect. That is why rioting does not take place in the better neighborhoods. Is it not in the white man's own interest to find a way to help the black man to his fair share?

The easiest way to give the Negro a stake is to offer him the same incentives offered most whites. There is no reason to work hard for a diploma if it is a passport to nowhere. There is no reason to work hard if promotions are off-limits.

Profit sharing is a method companies are employing to increase employee incentive. Some companies even give beginning workers some shares of its stock so that they will feel they are the company and will, thereby, work harder. Negroes should be offered these same opportunities, preferentially, so that they can be convinced the company is in earnest. Since they have been forced back, they must be pulled forward so that they can start on equal ground. Golfers are given handicaps to equalize competition and so are horses. Need we look to sports for examples of just treatment in America?

A guaranteed income at a liveable level would make Negroes part owners of the country. Most men would seek to protect an economy which makes a guaranteed living possible. They wouldn't want to destroy a vehicle which can put food in their babies' mouths even if times are bad. A man who shares the toil but not the profit is an embittered man. Give each American his share and a few crying "Revolt!" will be ignored.

REDISTRIBUTION OF POPULATION

In 1965, Negroes represented 66 per cent of the population of Washington, D.C., 34 per cent of Cleveland, 28 per cent of Chicago, 34 per cent of Detroit. This is an increase of 88 per cent in Washington, 113 per cent in Cleveland, 50 per cent in Chicago and 113 per cent in Detroit in just fifteen years.[8] As ghettos increase in numbers and size, so does discrimination against Negroes, for it is easier to discriminate against a group than against an individual. Society does not isolate so that it can build a fence around the problem. The best way to lessen discrimination, therefore, is to decentralize the problem. Only in this way will the Negro ever hope to gain an equal voice and stake in this land.

One approach which would help to achieve this end is altering the present patterns of migration, thus taking care of one segment of the problem for the future. This is not to suggest that the government should restrict the flow of migration into Washington, Baltimore, Cleveland or Detroit. There is no way the government can or should prevent people from moving, if they so desire. Nor should the government adopt the inhumane tactics used by some cities to try and halt the flow, such as the enactment of residency laws for welfare and other types of assistance. This is punitive treatment and more punishment is not needed. Furthermore, such tactics don't stop people from coming in anyway, for few check the welfare regulations in a city before going there. Such laws just penalize them when they arrive and increase an already crippling burden for a period of a year.

What America must do is make it desirable for people to be elsewhere. For precedent it has just to reach back into its own history to the days of the Wild West when its leaders wanted people to leave the East and expand its frontiers. The government encouraged Americans to move into new parts of the country with vigorous campaigns which appealed to the pioneer spirit. It glamorized the West and made travellers into folk heroes.

The country even went further. In 1862 Congress passed the Homestead Act, making available one hundred sixty acres of free farmland to any citizen or applicant for citizenship who would agree to cultivate the land for a period of five years. In 1873, it passed the Timber Culture Act which gave the settler an additional hundred and sixty acres of relatively treeless land if he was willing to plant trees on at least a quarter of it within four years. And in 1877, Congress passed the Desert Land Act which allowed frontiersmen to acquire six hundred forty acres for twenty-five cents an acre down and a promise to irrigate the land within a three-year period.

The same approach adopted today could lessen traffic into the urban North and could decongest the already overpopulated city street. Indeed, it might find many enthusiasts among city dwellers because there is little that is not ugly in their lives. Birth control is not the only method to control the population explosion which helps to cause blight in the city. Its powers are limited, for it cannot do anything about the people who are already here. Urban renewal can't either, although the country's leaders would like to think it can. All urban renewal can do is help shuffle people around on the same land. To date it has created more problems than it has alleviated, for it has intensified ghettos. It has closed down one area after another to the poor. Even fair housing laws won't end the problem. The fair housing legislation will open up more housing to Negroes as it ends discrimination, but it will not add to the total housing supply. It will make the total supply more equally available and this will unquestionably relieve the problem. It won't solve it, however, for there will remain a pressing need for low- and moderate-income housing.

When America thinks in terms of population resettlement, it must think in terms of mixing up the whole population—black and white. But the path can be cleared only by industry and government. It is government's responsibility to turn over land it owns to the construction of integrated communities after attracting industry to build plants nearby. It is industry's responsibility to provide jobs and job training for all segments of the population, for only through such efforts can integration work.

By building up the highways and byways of America which are vacant now, population and racial redistribution could become a reality. In urban areas, this means using suburbia's open spaces. Suburbia still has land. It has some new and uncrowded schools. There is room for industry; there is room for new housing. Suburbia has heretofore worked hard to keep out all it views as evil. It consciously and actively seeks separation, isolation, segregation. But this is 1968 and isolationism can't work. People are talking about metropolitan planning because they realize that the suburb needs the city perhaps more than the city needs the suburb. Why else have metropolitan approaches in transportation and water been adopted? Why else is white middle-class America so threatened by city riots? The cities are the lifeline of the suburbs. Suburbs cannot thrive unless cities survive. No matter how beautiful the body, when the heart stops the body begins to disintegrate.

To date, the suburbs have taken, but they have obdurately refused to give. Most cities have given, and most are beginning to show the strain. They are getting impatient. There are city administrations which have not buckled and which have forced the suburbs to cooperate by threatening to discontinue their water supply. Such action is to be applauded and will probably increase now that success has been tasted. Cities can well demand that suburbia take its share of the lower-income population, its share of industry, its share of the minority population, its share of the metropolitan responsibility in return for all the services that the city provides. Suburbia will find that cooperating with the city in these ways will be to its own advantage. It will increase the supply of skilled and unskilled labor for suburban industry and services, and it will help strengthen the city without weakening the suburbs. It will thereby breathe a new and wholesome vitality into an entire metropolitan area.

In rural areas where land is even more plentiful, population redistribution can be achieved by encouraging industrial development. The urban-suburban conflict won't have to be dealt with. But greater incentives need to be offered to encourage people to move farther distances. Transportation allowances would be a necessity, and promises of more training, better housing for less money and greater chances of advancement are the least that can be offered.

Doubters will claim that people won't agree to be uprooted in this way, especially if the job opportunities are not close by. And it is true that some will always choose the known, however dismal, over the unknown, however promising it may be. But many will take the risk. People now go across the country to follow a job, to follow an inheritance, to get an education, to get a job. If individuals are rewarded for moving with better living conditions and with a life unstigmatized by ghetto walls, they will leave the cities the same way they left Alabama and Mississippi when they faced a hard, cold trek northward with nothing but hope and little of that.

Large American companies move plants and plant employees as a matter of course. Oftentimes, when plants are constructed, so are industrial communities. Industries subsidize the financing of homes. There is no reason why industry can't use the same technique it is already engaged in to help solve the country's major problem. If a respected American company will provide the jobs and training, if racial balances are maintained, if new, uncrowded schools are opened, Negroes and whites will move.

Industry is decentralizing its operations anyway. With a boost from government, what appears idealistic and utopian could become a reality. Government could well offer incentives such as tax-write-downs to cooperating companies. It could make land available at low prices. It could offer special Federal training programs.

There are others who will doubt and even resist such a program because they feel greater protection in numbers. They need comfort—they want to feel wanted. In the ghetto they have friends. A few of their numbers care. The walls protect. What they choose is to remain behind the line of scrimmage. As long as a player is behind the line of scrimmage, he is affected only by his own teammates; it is only as he crosses the line that he is exposed to the other side, the enemy. Some rationalize that as long as they can run around back there, there is no need to risk moving.

Yet man really can't run around behind the line anymore. There is no space. There is no air. Children are starving. So he must penetrate the wall and face the uncertainties, the opposition on the other side. No one can promise heaven. All one can guarantee is an escape from hell.

American leaders must build the same kind of mixes into the heart of the city that have been proposed above for suburban and rural areas. Many think integration in Washington is impossible because the percentage of blacks is so great. Yet they admit there is value in integration. If that is the case, then city planners must work to achieve it. How? By changing the percentages, by building a different kind of population mix in the city. And if they succeed in resettling many city dwellers, they will open up cities again to some who reside in the suburbs. In so doing they will not only achieve a greater racial distribution, they will also achieve greater economic and social diversity.

COMMUNICATION IS THE KEY

The white American sees the black man as a burden, a burden which is growing heavier and heavier all the time. And so the white American responds as he has been responding for three centuries by trying to see how he can lessen the weight, assuming all the while that he is still going to have to shoulder it. And so he prays:

> This is my burden and I must bear it, oh Lord, but don't let me carry it too far or too long at one time. When I rest, hide it from me so that I need not feel troubled; I will pick it up again, carry it still further, but let it breathe lightly all the while, for I am so weary.

How strange and how pathetic! What danger there is in making assumptions based upon inaccuracies. The Negro is not asking to be carried. He has never asked to be carried. All he asks is the chance to get up on his feet without being knocked over again.

There has always been this total lack of communication between the races in America. As Ralph Ellison said, "I would like to hear fewer theories spun out about what I am when I am right here to be talked to, to be observed, to be visited, if one so desires."[9] And there will continue to be no communication until the two races deal with each other directly in the same classrooms, in the same offices, on the same playgrounds, on the same dance floors, and in the same neighborhoods. Without communication we will continue to spend millions of dollars on programs and plans which offer new schemes but which repeat old errors. With no communication the real problems will never get attacked. With no communication, riots, if not open rebellion, are inevitable and dangerously near.

As long as there are ghetto walls, be they invisible or not, there can be no communication between those within and those without. Dialogue can never penetrate walls of concrete, years of anguished separation. If the walls don't come down, the cities will. The black world has tried to tell the white world its intentions—should the white world continue to play deaf, it will become a victim of its own game.

7

After the Fire

It was the best of times, it was the worst of times. . . .[1]

—CHARLES DICKENS

The America of the late 1960's is repulsed by militant cries, mesmerized by unfulfilled promises, frayed from acts of anarchy, rewoven by hands unsure of their mission, convulsed in spasms of hatred, sedated by hymns of love. The country wants to act, but it is also willing to be acted upon. It wants to be a nation indivisible, yet it gives separation and segregation the sanctity of law. It wants to hold high the beacon of freedom, yet it blindfolds some of its citizenry lest they see the beams.

America's wracking inconsistencies and contradictions have unsteadied its population. They have raised suspicion and distrust in other parts of the world. Americans are no longer sure what their country is, nor do they know what it will become. Other nations have scrutinized its self-righteous pronouncements; they increasingly ridicule its high-sounding ideals.

Yet America continues to forge ahead, rewarding whites for the color of their skin, punishing blacks for the color of theirs; rewarding the suburbanite for fleeing the city, taxing and re-taxing the city dweller for his inability to jump the wall. The country is opting to continue running nowhere. It refuses to slow down or stop so that it might regroup its forces and garner new strength. Motion seems to be its own excuse.

Can this America understand the real issues? Does it see that what is on trial in the battle for the city is the future of democracy? Can it understand that its actions will determine whether or not democracy can work, whether freedom is but an empty hope for all but the middle and upper classes who ride to glory on the calloused backs of the poor?

During the period of Reconstruction the South became a somewhat integrated society. Two Southern Negroes took seats in the United States Senate, twenty-one Negroes from the South were elected to the House of Representatives.[2] At the State and local levels, many Negroes held public office and a few became important figures in public life.[3] Intermarriage was not outlawed.

The South's apparent open-mindedness lasted for a period of only a few years. Then Jim Crow began to reappear and with it came the admission that democracy couldn't work. Perhaps such an admission was easy in the late 1800's, for the country enjoyed a position of relative isolation.

But the question that rankles today is whether America is willing to make that same admission in 1969 and 1970. If not, it had better begin to produce some evidence to the contrary, for it is no longer easy to fool other nations by mouthing empty "save-democracy-the-world-over" clichés when America's own waters are poisoned with bigotry and racism. The world has decreased in size, and it is no longer possible to control the proliferation of news, try as we may. Nor is it possible to fool those who are the oppressed at home. They know better than any the difference between the word and the act. They are on to the system's brutal game.

If American democracy is to survive, the country must resolve old dilemmas. It must be willing to move beyond the promise of equal opportunity to the actual provision of equal results. It must revamp its existing structures to satisfy the needs of the poor, if it wishes to retain the old structures at all. It must accept the hard fact that its hand has been forced, that there are but two choices remaining—to act or to be destroyed. It must lead its citizenry to realize that what is good for Negroes is good for whites, that in crippling one segment of society it cripples all of society. It must decide ultimately to eliminate its ghettos, to draw up immediate plans to tear down ghetto walls. And, while planning for tomorrow, it must make life in the ghetto worth living today. It must share power and it must share profit. It must be prepared for a real showdown on issues that count.

It can't go on trying to solve problems by buying off a few of the potential bomb throwers. Pay-offs work only until the payee gets smart and sees that he is being used.

HOW WILL THE NEGRO USE HIS POWER?

The Negro citizen faces a dilemma he must resolve—how to use his growing numbers and increasing power creatively to get what he wants. In the 1964 national elections, the National Urban League ran a voter registration campaign and found that the Negro was the balance of power in the election. If the Negro populations in just eighteen cities united in a bloc and voted in concert, they could swing an entire national election. While it is obvious that all black men will never unite and vote in a bloc, the point is mentioned as an indicator of black potential power. Already Cleveland, Gary, and Washington, D.C., have black men heading their city governments. In the South, in racially reactionary Mississippi, Negroes were able to elect twenty-two blacks to office, including one state representative and four county supervisors. White politicians nationwide are growing fearful and are looking for ways to dilute the power of the Negro at the polls.

But the black man can't yet begin to feel complacent, because numbers alone don't necessarily bring greater economic strength. They don't automatically produce better schools, better housing, more meaningful jobs. But numbers can do all these things, if they do not work at cross-purposes with their own.

Many will argue that metropolitan government and population dispersal are bad for the Negro, for they will dilute his strength. But they dilute his strength only as he allows them to. As city, State and Federal governments move to encourage metropolitan planning and population dispersal, the Negro needs to use his numbers and his strength to get some seats on the boards that make the basic decisions about what the programs would do, how they would function, and who would wield the power. Before old structures give way to new, while his strength is still centralized, the Negro must use that strength and power to write himself into the future.

The challenge and the dilemma the black man faces are precisely how to get what he needs—metropolitan government and population dispersal—without sacrificing power. If he uses his numbers to defeat these concepts, reasoning that such devices would rid him of his political strength, he will find himself a victim of his own logic, for there is little strength in starvation and unemployment, however great the numbers.

If blacks with all their numbers fight to take over Newark, a city struggling hard to survive, they would sanction the suburbs to build shops, schools and roads around them. Whites would proceed to tighten the noose already around the ghetto's neck and strangle the black man with all his numbers, right in the heart of his own city. Wouldn't it be wiser for blacks to use their numbers to make the metropolitan area of Newark more viable for everyone, especially themselves?

Power is like money. It has value only when it is used wisely. Millions of dollars buried in the ground won't do anybody any good. But if the money is extracted from the earth and put to good use, it will produce some kind of change, some kind of reward.

If the black man in Newark, or any other central city, chooses to remain seated on a chest full of gold with his eyes closed to all that goes on outside his purview, someone might just succeed in boring a hole in the bottom of the chest, draining out the gold and carrying it into the suburbs. The man on the chest will someday awaken to reality—to the fact that his chest isn't worth very much in and of itself.

The Negro masses face another dilemma that seems equally perplexing—how to move from being a weapon to being a tool. Over the past few years, through the direct action activities of numerous civil rights groups and through the rioting in the cities, blacks have been clamoring for the attention of their country. They now have the attention they sought. There is no need to seek it any longer; activism and destructiveness cannot be their own excuses, for in and of themselves, they accomplish little. Now that the spotlight is beaming their way, blacks must produce change, and they must produce it quickly, for the national attention span is very short. Negroes need no longer use up their energy on angry destructiveness. There's too much work to be done and the night is coming; there's more to be harvested and laborers are too few.

NEED FOR CONTINUING REAPPRAISAL

The Negro leader needs to take a long, hard and honest look at himself. He must realize that new questions require new answers, changing times require changing methodology. Obviously, it can't be business as usual. Approaches that were needed and accepted and productive just five short years ago are today utterly invalid. Yesterday there was a need for the one or two strong, controlling and compelling Negro leaders who could rally mass support in the fight for important legislation. When war raged at the national level, the national figure and the national organization were important. Today, there is no one war. Small battles are flaring in cities as different as Cambridge, Maryland, and Detroit, Michigan. Mass support is there—someone is needed to gather it together, not to control it. The man who strikes a responsive chord in Cambridge might find only a handful of followers in urban, urbane Detroit.

Today there is a need for numerous leaders—for men who want to work *for* their people, not on or over their people, for men who seek to talk for their people rather than at them, for men who can move with the problems, not around them.

The Negro leader who today is to remain relevant has to be on the side of those who are poor and in need. And, should it come to the point of choosing up sides, the black leader must find himself supporting the black masses, whatever the price. The source of his financing or other support cannot determine which way he leans. This does not mean that if the masses are crying revolution, he needs to help blow up the town. But it does mean that he must assess, as selflessly as is humanly possible, what action on his part would best serve the interest of his people and then act accordingly.

Negro leaders must realize the danger in perpetuating stereotypes. Negroes probably know better than any other group in America that generalizations about a people or a group refer to only some individuals in that group and that all group members are not responsible for the actions of the few.

The Jew has lately become the target of repeated attacks by black militant leaders. And while it is true that some Jewish businessmen and landlords ruthlessly exploit the ghetto resident, it is equally true that many Jewish people are, and have been, the strongest civil rights proponents and civil rights activists in the white community. While some Jews are the Negro's greatest oppressors in America, others are the Negro's sincerest friends. By perpetuating a stereotype that brands all Jews because of the sins of the few, black militants may well destroy the strongest group support the Negro has in white America. This would undoubtedly be self-defeating.

While it is unfair for blacks to judge the leadership of the Jewish community or to damn Jews in general for the actions of the individual Jew who milks the ghetto, the leaders of the Jewish community should not be distracted by angry cries from a few isolated corners. Rather, they should continue to attack *all* exploiters of the black man, attack *all* who continue to starve the ghetto, for that is the surest way to help blacks fight exploitation and quiet irrational, embittered voices.

The Negro leadership at present is confused and at war with itself. In the past it fought hard to clear the paths it now walks. In the battles to get out of the wilderness, each leader, each organization, trod a path which promised to lead to salvation. The harder the work, the surer the goal. The thicker the sweat, the more convincing the cause. Down one path came revolutionary cries, from another came pleas for black unity and black strength, from still another came cries for more understanding, more patience, more time.

Today, each path still has its warriors; each warrior has a creed and the tools he thinks he needs to forge ahead. But, so far, the paths have meandered in separate directions. Each warring group has purposefully avoided the crossroads for fear of the conflict which might ensue. Few care to force confrontation, for some sacrifices would be required of each if all were to join peacefully in one large crusade. Each group opts to go it alone, reasoning or rationalizing that it can't risk undoing what it has accomplished over the years, that it can't afford to take two steps back, even if the end result might be three steps forward. It is as if the means have become ends in themselves. The ultimate goal—unity, equality, freedom—has become lost somewhere along the way.

Black leaders need to accept the fact that differing philosophies, differing approaches, exist. None can be wished away or washed away. Many have tried to muddy the paths of adversaries. But none has succeeded in stopping a march, for each cause has its avid advocates who will endure.

The moderate civil rights leaders, despite their relative security in American society, cannot succeed in restraining the black power militants, and they would be wise to stop trying and start listening. Black power advocates have come up with a good strategy. Negroes *should* be pooling their resources to provide jobs for other Negroes, even though the pooling of resources is but a first step toward unity and not an answer in and of itself. Negroes *should* be seeking to provide training for their brothers; they *should* be anxious to start black businesses, to bid for the Negro market; they *should* be given some control over their all-black schools; they *should* have a hand in policing their own neighborhoods. Black power has been a motivating force. It has given Negroes a little courage when courage seemed all used up. The dynamism of the black power leaders and their pride-provoking words and acts have helped the Negro in the ghetto face life.

Similarly, the black power advocates must live with the moderate elements of black society. Blacks who are out to shoot down traditional leaders will find that when and if they succeed, the same problems will remain, for in silencing one or two voices of moderation, they would silence but one or two voices—not moderation itself, no matter how many bullets hit home.

And moderates *have* met many successes over the years. They have helped to open up public accommodations to blacks; they have helped to increase the size of the Negro electorate by fighting for the passage of the Voting Rights Act; they have increased job and training opportunities for Negro men and women; they have won many courtroom battles, thereby gaining increasing protection for blacks.

Black militants need realize that they have only a piece of the solution and that the answer to the complex problems of the

American black man is not in their hands alone. Indeed, the future of the black man in America is not in the hands of any one group or any one leader. No organization has a monopoly on workable solutions. No group has found "the" answer, because there is no *one* answer, no *one* wise man. The white man has scored too many points by forcing the black man to strangle his own brothers. Unless blacks can unite against the real enemy, their efforts will remain paralyzed and suicidal. By carrying on their own private wars against each other, black leaders are wasting needed energy and resources. They are attaching a new set of chains to their own legs.

There are many Negroes who remain unsympathetic to both the black power advocates and the integrationists. They see black power as a road to separation, and they are convinced that separation is unfeasible for the black man because he does not have the resources and the power which would enable him to use that separation to his own advantage. Integration, too, is rejected as a solution because in America integration has degraded and humiliated the black man. Integration, as defined and practiced in this country, asks the Negro to reject his past. It tells the black man that he *might* be able to mingle if he models himself after the white man.

Those blacks seeking integration in America are asking something of someone else. They seem to be pounding on white doors, asking, indeed pleading, for admittance to a house they helped build, a house they should have the right to enter. Integration allows the white man the luxury of making the choice. He can choose to open the door or bolt it closed. His whim is the black man's destiny.

Integration, as it is presently practiced, is a white man's handout. It is not a sharing process. It is a granting process. Blacks and whites do not partake equally—blacks share what whites allow them to share. Few black men really benefit.

As the rift between the black power advocates and the integrationists has widened, it has been increasingly difficult to keep one foot in each camp. For if one accepts a part of the black power philosophy, one is labeled a militant. He who believes the 1954 Supreme Court decision is labeled a "sell-out to integration." The person who opposes separation and who at the same time sees the ghetto as a present and destructive reality and advocates black control to ameliorate the situation is *ipso facto* a black power advocate.

We need to stop playing semantic games. Labels are meaningless and dangerous because they oversimplify and distort, because they kill thought. They encourage people to take shortcuts, to read labels instead of studying and analyzing the substance of the material or the idea.

The only solution lies in a combination of both approaches. Consistency is not the goal. True equality is. If we reject a part of a comprehensive solution in an attempt to be 100 per cent consistent, we will knock ourselves out, and for all the wrong reasons. The goal is a single society wherein a man gives according to his ability and none receives less than his need. To reach this goal, different approaches are needed.

Black power advocates have neither the means nor the numbers to get blacks what they deserve. Though the black man's blood and the blood of his ancestors have been strewn from Bunker Hill to Vietnam, most black Americans still do not seek to redress past and present grievances by the sword. Likewise, black integrationists can accomplish little by themselves, for they are not moving from strength. They can take only when they are given, and that isn't taking.

The only solution is in a wider definition of integration—perhaps a *new* definition for white America. Integration is not a passing gesture, a few thousand new jobs, more liberal welfare regulations. Integration is the *full* partnership of black and white. It is the redistribution of capital, resources, and power. Integration means white sacrifice. If whites believe democracy can work, they must believe in it enough to make it work. And democracy can survive only if whites choose to stand on their own two feet by refusing to ride to victory on the backs of blacks.

Negroes are ready to stand tall once the weight of oppression is lifted from their bodies. Can whites stand tall when their bolsters are removed?

DILEMMA OF THE CHURCH AND THE WHITE LIBERAL

The Church of the late 1960's finds itself with one of the greatest dilemmas of the day. It is trying to relate to the problems of the city only in theological terms because it is afraid to take a stand in the streets. Consequently, it is finding that its preaching goes unheeded, its answers seem sterile, its voice is being drowned out by cries which are truly arousing the ghetto.

Ever since the March on Washington in 1963 the Church has grown more conservative. As the action of the militants has been stepped up, the Church has moved back inside. It seems to have abandoned the cause of civil rights because a few radicals have entered the scene.

The clergy, if it is to remain creditable, cannot go on avoiding the main issues of the day. It cannot wish away the militants or secretly harbor hopes that such leaders will be jailed. Unless the central issues are solved, it matters little how many militants are put behind bars, because more and more waves of them will roll in. It mustn't be forgotten that the militants did not create the situation in the slums—the slums created the militants.

The violence in the city challenges the established Church. The more defensive the stance the clergy takes, and the longer it hides in its theology, the more it will discredit itself.

The white liberal, like the Church, has found himself beset with new problems, problems which have forced him to reexamine his beliefs, his real motivation, and to reassess the depths of his commitment. Who is he and what does he really want?

The white liberal is beginning to understand that what he thought was the problem in American race relations isn't the problem at all, because he thought the problem didn't include him. It was the other whites who impeded progress. He was home free. He really didn't care if a Negro moved into his neighborhood. All that concerned him was property values. He really didn't mind if Negro children went to school with his kids, but he wasn't going to permit *anyone* to lower the quality of education in his schools! The militants have forced the liberal to see that his skepticism over integration in housing and education, for whatever reasons, is the same skepticism evidenced by the out-and-out bigot. And the skepticism of the liberal is even more damaging to the Negro because it is whispered in loving tones.

The black American allowed the white man the luxury of thinking himself a liberal for too long. Intellectual understandings of the issues were seldom challenged. In the absence of real tests, it was easy to talk. Today, the liberal has been called upon to prove his worth and his commitment and to live his ideas and ideals. He is still wanted and needed in the front lines of the battle, yet he is subjected to the increasing scrutiny of others, his advice goes unheeded, his answers are often disregarded or treated with scorn. But in days when most things white are distrusted, in days when black hatred for white has moved from a series of individual dislikes to a generalized hatred of whiteness, the liberal needs to be prepared to deal with the hostility his white face provokes, and in order to do so, he needs to understand the reason for that hatred.

The man truly interested in civil rights, black rights and integration, understanding the prolonged history of racism in America, will know why blacks are frustrated and incensed. Consequently, he won't feel threatened by a few anti-white cries. He won't let the anger of the few sidetrack him. He will see that he still has an important role to play in the civil rights movement and he will proceed with the real work at hand. He will work to achieve integration on both sides of the opaque wall. He will work for fair housing laws; he will attempt to convince his neighbors to sell or rent their homes to Negroes. He will push for integration in the schools; he'll work for bussing programs. He will lobby for a stronger Negro voice, increased Negro control, deeper and more pervasive black influence.

He'll join civil rights organizations that will be glad to welcome him, even if he can't lead them. Organizations like the Urban League, the Southern Christian Leadership Conference and the National Association for the Advancement of Colored People welcome any and all who are willing to take up the mantle and run with the cause.

But the man who backs out, feeling rejected by the increased animosity aimed at him and his kind, ought to examine his motivation. If he truly is interested in making democracy work, he can't allow a few personal affronts to affect his attitude toward, and his involvement in, causes he knows to be right and just. In backing out, he only helps the radicals prove that the white man will run when he can't lead and patronize others. In backing out, he teaches the black man that it is better not to trust whites, for in tough times that trust may well be betrayed.

For too long, Americans who pride themselves on being fair-minded have rationalized away their inactivity in matters racial by claiming that they, alone, can't change a corrupt and unjust system. And so, instead of seeking to change what they can, they opt for silence, inactivity, and isolation.

Such citizens can no longer be allowed the luxury of painting themselves noble. Their actions belie any personal integrity. Any man who does not oppose a corrupt system becomes an agent for that system, regardless of whether or not he actually affirms it. In not speaking out and working against injustices, he aids and abets those injustices.

Furthermore, the man who institutionalizes his relationships is responsible for the resultant institution and should be judged accordingly. The realtor who joins the National Association of Real Estate Boards is responsible for the policies and practices of that institution. The clergyman is responsible for the pronouncements of his Church. The businessman can't pat himself on the back for not agreeing with the policies of the businessman's association if he is a member of the association. Americans have been hiding behind the organizations and the institutions they support for years. It is time to challenge those who sit on both sides of the fence, gaining prestige from membership in an organization and moral fortitude from privately dissociating themselves from the practices of the organization. As long as one remains in an organization, he is that organization.

GOVERNMENT MUST REASSESS

Government officials, too, need realize that their inactivity hurts them and their nation. It swells the ranks of the rioters. The power structure can no longer punish black people into obedience. It needs to act positively, and if it remains unwilling to deal meaningfully with the Clarence Mitchells, it will have to deal with the militants—and not on its terms.

Congress seems to think it can continue to function as a nice little club neatly tucked away in a carefully guarded and protected corner of the nation's Capitol. But it can't. The black star is rising. As blacks and their supporters gain politically, each national officeholder will be forced to pull his head out of the sand. And if the time comes when a Senator Eastland has a choice between voting in support of civil rights legislation or giving up his seat in Congress, there seems little doubt but that he would choose the former, because he loves the Senate of the United States more than he loves segregation. Segregation is not only a moral and ethical question. It is political as well.

Government, along with white America, must become a little less preoccupied with four or five Negroes. Over the past year, the government has been so busy trying to dispose of Adam Clayton Powell, Stokely Carmichael, Rap Brown, and Cassius Clay that it has failed to look at the real issues that are boiling over a hot flame.

The Bible states in one of its Scriptures that it won't be water, but fire next time. This, of course, relates to the first time God became angry with man and told Noah to gather up his family and the animals from the field, two by two, to build an ark and lead the chosen in. After forty days and forty nights of ceaseless rain washed away most of mankind, the Lord reminded Noah that it won't be water, but fire next time.

Are we not witnessing the prophesied fire? It seems to be a time for burning. Summer after summer the skies bleed; summers are beginning to stretch into years. Cities have been wracked apart. Neighbor has turned against neighbor. Lives have been charred from within and without. Inhumanity, insensitivity, brutality, and bestiality abound. Will we survive these forty days and forty nights of fire?

First water. Then fire. What will it be next time?

Notes

INTRODUCTION

1. William McGaffin and Erwin Knoll, "The White House Lies," *The Progressive,* September 1967, p. 13.

Chapter 1

1. U.S. Congress, Senate, Committee on Government Operations, *Federal Role in Urban Affairs, Hearings,* before the Subcommittee on Executive Reorganization of the Committee on Government Operations, Part 5, Senate, 89th Cong., 2nd sess., 1966, p. 1095.
2. "Report of the Advisory Committtee of the Service to Displaced Families to the Director of Public Welfare at the Expiration of the Six Months Trial Period, March 21, 1960 to September 20, 1960," Department of Public Welfare, Public Assistance Division, Washington, D.C. (mimeographed).
3. Dagmar Horna Perman, *The Girard Street Project* (Washington, D.C.: All Souls Church Unitarian, 1964).
4. Byrone E. Calame, "Rent Control: It's Welfare in Disguise," *Wall Street Journal,* March 13, 1967, p. 12.
5. Hubert Humphrey, Address at Conference of National League of Cities, Boston, July 31, 1967, quoted in *The States and Urban Problems: A Staff Study for the Committee on State-Urban Relations of the National Governors' Conference,* 1967, p. 61.
6. Ellis D. Sox, Address to the American Public Health Association, Annual Meeting, 1964, *Public Health Reports,* LXXX, 2 (February 1965), p. 100.
7. The Girard Street Association was created in 1963 under the sponsorship of the Social Welfare Committee of All Souls Church Unitarian, Washington, D.C. Comprised of residents of the Girard Street area, a run-down, inner-city neighborhood, it functioned as a community-service and community-action organization. It has now been incorporated into the Columbia Heights Church Community Project.
8. Perman, *op. cit.*
9. Carl Bernstein, "City Housing Office Declines to Aid Crackdown on Major Slum Landlords," *Washington Post,* October 17, 1967, p. A1.
10. President's Commission on Law Enforcement and Administration of Justice, *Task Force: The Courts* (Washington, D.C.: Government Printing Office, 1967), p. 50.
11. Hobson v. Hansen, 269-F. SUPP. 401 (1967), reprinted in *Congressional Record,* June 21, 1967, p. H7665.

12. "Statement of Paul W. Briggs, Superintendent of Schools, Cleveland, Ohio," *Hearing Before the United States Commission on Civil Rights, Cleveland, Ohio,* April 1-7, 1966, p. 775.
13. Hobson v. Hansen, p. H7667.
14. Pride was formed in Washington, D.C., during the summer of 1967. It employed young men from the ghetto to clean up slum streets and carried on an extensive program of rat extermination. Chapters 1 and 6.
15. U.S. Department of Health, Education, and Welfare, *Equality of Educational Opportunity,* by James S. Coleman, et al. (Washington, D.C.: Government Printing Office, 1966), p. 223.
16. Commission on Civil Rights, *Racial Isolation in the Public Schools,* Vol. 1 (Washington, D.C.: Government Printing Office, 1967), p. 74.
17. Antoine de Saint-Exupery. *The Little Prince,* trans. by Katherine Woods (New York: Harcourt, Brace & World, 1943), p. 38.
18. *Federal Role in Urban Affairs,* Part 6, p. 1257.
19. *Wall Street Journal,* August 16, 1966, p. 8.
20. U.S. Federal Trade Commission, *Economic Report on Installment Credit and Retail Sales Practices of District of Columbia Retailers,* Washington, D.C., March 1968, p. 43.
21. Donald J. Black and Albert J. Reiss, "Patterns of Behavior in Police and Citizen Transactions," *Studies in Crime and Law Enforcement in Major Metropolitan Areas,* President's Commission on Law Enforcement and Administration of Justice, Field Survey III (Washington, D.C.: Government Printing Office, 1967), p. 136.
22. Bruce J. Terris, "The Role of the Police," *The Annals of the American Academy of Political and Social Science,* CCCLXXIV (November 1967), p. 66.
23. Anon, quoted in Kenneth B. Clark, p. 4.
24. St. Clair Drake, "The Social and Economic Status of the Negro in the United States," in *The Negro American,* ed. by Talcott Parsons and Kenneth B. Clark (Boston: Beacon Press, 1966), p. 27.
25. Harlem Youth Opportunities Unlimited, Inc., *Youth in the Ghetto: A Study of the Consequences of Powerlessness and a Blueprint for Change* (New York: Harlem Youth Opportunities Unlimited, Inc., 1964), p. 100.
26. "Towards a Social Geography of Health, Welfare and Recreation Facilities and Services in the District of Columbia," Health and Welfare Council of the National Capital Area, Washington, D.C., 1965, pp. 9, 12.
27. National Advisory Commission on Civil Disorders, *Report of the National Advisory Commission on Civil Disorders,* Bantam Books (New York: The New York Times Company, 1968), p. 1.

Chapter 2

1. Albert Camus, "The Myth of Sisyphus," trans. by Justin O'Brien in *The Myth of Sisyphus and Other Essays,* Vintage Books (New York: Random House, 1955), p. 88.
2. Ossie Davis, "The English Language is My Enemy!" *Negro History Bulletin,* XXX, 4 (April 1967), p. 18.
3. Kenneth B. Clark and Mamie P. Clark, "Racial Identification and

Preference in Negro Children," in *Readings in Social Psychology,* ed. by T. M. Newcomb and E. L. Hartley (New York: Henry Holt and Co., 1947, pp. 169-78.

4. Mary Ellen Goodman, "Evidence Concerning the Genesis of Interracial Attitudes," *American Anthropologist,* XLVIII (1946), pp. 624-30.
5. Mary Ellen Goodman, *Race Awareness in Young Children,* new rev. ed. (New York: Collier Books; London: Collier-Macmillan Ltd., 1964), p. 245.
6. Arthur W. Combs, "A Perceptual View of the Adequate Personality," *Perceiving, Behaving, Becoming: A New Focus for Education,* 1962 Yearbook of the Association for Supervision and Curriculum Development (Washington, D.C.: National Education Association, 1962), p. 53.
7. Earl C. Kelley, "The Fully Functioning Self," *Perceiving, Behaving, Becoming,* p. 15.
8. St. Clair Drake, "The Social and Economic Status of the Negro in the United States," in *The Negro American,* ed. by Talcott Parsons and Kenneth B. Clark (Boston: Beacon Press, 1966), p. 36.
9. Samuel D. Proctor, *The Young Negro in America, 1960-1980* (New York: Association Press, 1966), p. 52.
10. Ralph Ellison, *Invisible Man* (New York: Random House, 1952), p. 434.
11. Dorothy Sterling, *Forever Free: The Story of the Emancipation Proclamation* (Garden City, New York: Doubleday & Co., Inc., 1963), p. 196.
12. Harold H. Eibling et al., *History of Our United States,* 2nd ed. (Summit, New Jersey: Laidlow Brothers, Publishers, a division of Doubleday & Co., Inc., 1966), p. 11.
13. Robert P. Ludlum et al., *American Government* (Boston: Houghton Mifflin Company, 1965), p. 14.
14. Robert Rienow, *The Citizen and His Government: Rights and Responsibilities* (Boston: Houghton Mifflin Company, 1967), pp. 8, 9.
15. E. Franklin Frazier, *The Negro in the United States,* rev. ed. (New York: The Macmillan Company, 1957), p. 127.
16. Plessy v. Ferguson, 163 U.S. 537 (1896), reprinted in *The Supreme Court on Racial Discrimination,* ed. by Joseph Tussman (New York: Oxford University Press, 1963), p. 65.
17. Ibid., pp. 68, 74.
18. Rayford W. Logan, *The Negro in American Life and Thought* (New York: Dial Press, Inc., 1954), pp. ix-x.
19. Brown v. Board of Education, 347 U.S. 483 (1954), reprinted in *The Supreme Court on Racial Discrimination,* p. 42.
20. Anon., quoted in James Baldwin, "A Negro Assays the Negro Mood," *New York Times Magazine,* March 12, 1961, p. 103.
21. Bayard Rustin, "The Great Lessons of Birmingham," *Liberation,* VIII, 4 (June 1963), reprinted in *Negro Protest Thought in the Twentieth Century,* ed. by Francis L. Broderick and August Meier (New York: Bobbs-Merrill Company, Inc., 1965), p. 305.
22. Martin Luther King, "Letters from Birmingham City Jail" (Philadelphia: American Friends Service Committee, 1963), reprinted in *The Negro in Twentieth Century America: A Reader on the Struggle*

for Civil Rights, ed. by John Hope Franklin and Isidore Starr, Vintage Books (New York: Random House, 1967), pp. 157-58.

23. John O. Killens, "Explanation of the 'Black Psyche,'" *New York Times Magazine,* June 7, 1964, p. 42.
24. George Gillis, "I Am Black," in "poems comin' from a BLACK thing," comp. by Faythe Smith and Arthur Smith, Forum 66, June 1967 (mimeographed).

Chapter 3

1. Michael Harrington, *The Other America: Poverty in the United States* (New York: The Macmillan Company, 1964), p. 72.
2. Herbert S. Klein, *Slavery in the Americas: A Comparative Study of Virginia and Cuba* (Chicago: University of Chicago Press, 1967), p. 60.
3. William L. Schurz, *Brazil: The Infinite Country* (New York: E. P. Dutton & Co., 1961), p. 110.
4. Kenneth M. Stampp, *The Peculiar Institution: Slavery in the Ante-Bellum South,* Vintage Books (New York: Random House, 1956), p. 208.
5. Stanley M. Elkins, *Slavery: A Problem in American Institutional and Intellectual Life,* The Universal Library (New York: Grosset and Dunlap, 1963), pp. 113, 129.
6. Charles Silberman, *Crisis in Black and White,* Vintage Books (New York: Random House, 1964), p. 78.
7. *National Intelligencer* (Washington, D.C.), August 23, 1862, quoted in Robert S. Harper, *Lincoln and the Press* (New York: McGraw-Hill Book Company, Inc., 1951), p. 174.
8. Silberman, p. 165.
9. U.S. Department of Labor and U.S. Department of Commerce, *Social and Economic Conditions of Negroes in the United States,* BLS Report No. 332, Current Population Reports, Series P-23, No. 24 (Washington, D.C.: Government Printing Office, 1967), pp. 29, 15, 41, 49.
10. Sam P. Wiggins, *Higher Education in the South* (Berkeley, California: McCutchan Publishing Corporation, 1966), p. 273.
11. Frank Tannenbaum, *Slave and Citizen: The Negro in the Americas,* Vintage Books (New York: Random House, 1946), pp. 113-14.
12. Oscar Handlin, *The Uprooted: The Epic Story of the Great Migrations That Made the American People* (Boston: Little, Brown and Company, 1951), pp. 146-48, 151-52, 154-55.
13. Robert Conot, *Rivers of Blood, Years of Darkness* (New York: Bantam Books, Inc., 1967), p. 438.
14. Ibid.
15. U.S. Department of Labor, Manpower Administration, *Manpower Report of the President* (Washington, D.C.: Government Printing Office, 1967), p. 211.
16. U.S. Department of Commerce, Bureau of the Census, *Historical Statistics of the United States: Colonial Times to 1957* (Washington, D.C.: Government Printing Office, 1961), p. 74.
17. U.S. Department of Labor, Bureau of Labor Statistics, *Employment and Earnings: Monthly Report on the Labor Force,* XIV, 7 (January 1968), p. 47.

18. Max Ways, "The Deeper Shame of the Cities," *Fortune,* January 1968, pp. 205, 206.
19. *Historical Statistics of the United States,* p. 74.
20. *Employment and Earnings,* p. 47.
21. Conot, p. 441.
22. Nathan Glazer and Daniel Moynihan, *Beyond the Melting Pot: The Negroes, Puerto Ricans, Jews and Italians and Irish of New York City* (Cambridge: MIT Press and Harvard University Press, 1963), p. 32.
23. Bayard Rustin, "From Protest to Politics," *Commentary,* XXXIX, 2 (February 1965), reprinted in *Negro Protest Thought in the Twentieth Century,* ed. by Francis L. Broderick and August Meier (New York: Bobbs-Merrill Company, Inc., 1965), p. 410.
24. Howard V. Howard, 6 Jones N.C. 235 (1858), reprinted in Helen Tunnicliff Catterall, ed., *Judicial Cases Concerning American Slavery and the Negro,* Vol. I (Washington, D.C.: Carnegie Institution of Washington, 1929), p. 221.
25. Stampp, p. 198.
26. Conot, p. 441.

Chapter 4

1. John O. Killens, "Explanation of the 'Black Psyche,'" *New York Times Magazine,* June 7, 1964, p. 48.
2. Civil Rights Act of 1964, Title VI, reprinted in Stanley Fleishman and Sam Rosenwein, *The New Civil Rights Act—What it Means to You!* (Los Angeles: Blackstone Book Company, 1964), p. 134.
3. Figure released by United States Office of Education, National Center for Educational Statistics, December 1966.
4. U.S. Department of Labor, Bureau of Labor Statistics, "Employment of High School Graduates and Dropouts in 1965," cited in *The Racial Gap: 1955-1965, 1965-1975 in Income, Unemployment, Education, Health, Housing* (New York: National Urban League, Inc., 1967), p. 16.
5. Rashi Fein, "An Economic and Social Profile of the Negro American," in *The Negro American,* ed. by Talcott Parsons and Kenneth B. Clark (Boston: Beacon Press, 1966), p. 123.
6. Phillip M. Hauser, "Demographic Factors in the Integration of the Negro," *Daedalus,* XCIV, 4 (Fall 1965), p. 860.
7. Bernard E. Anderson, "Employment of Negroes in the Federal Government," *Monthly Labor Review* (October 1965), pp. 1222-27.
8. James R. Wetzel and Susan B. Holland, "Poverty Areas of Our Major Cities," *Monthly Labor Review* (October, 1966), p. 1108.
9. National Advisory Commission on Civil Disorders, *Report of the National Advisory Commission on Civil Disorders,* Bantam Books (New York: The New York Times Company, 1968), p. 140.
10. Thomas O'Hanlon, "The Case Against Unions," *Fortune* (January, 1968), p. 173.
11. Ibid.
12. Wonderlic Personnel Test, Form IV, question 17.
13. U.S. Department of Labor, Manpower Administration, *Dictionary of Occupational Titles,* Vol. 1, 3rd ed. (Washington, D.C.: Government Printing Office, 1965), p. 497.

14. U.S. Department of Commerce, Bureau of the Census, *Statistical Abstract of the United States: 1967,* 88th ed. (Washington, D.C.: Government Printing Office, 1967), p. 235.
15. S. M. Miller and Martin Rein, "The War on Poverty: Perspectives and Prospects," in *Poverty as a Public Issue,* ed. by Ben B. Seligman (New York: The Free Press; London: Collier-Macmillan Ltd., 1965), pp. 294-97.
16. O'Hanlon, p. 170.
17. Nicholas Gage, "Negroes Barred from 'Executive' Posts in Organized Rackets," *Wall Street Journal,* October 26, 1967, p. 1.
18. Wetzel and Holland, pp. 1108, 1105.
19. *The Racial Gap,* p. 36.
20. U.S. Department of Commerce, Bureau of Census, *U.S. Censuses of Population and Housing 1960,* Final Report, PHC (1)-82 (Washington, D.C.: Government Printing Office, 1962), Table H3; U.S. Department of Commerce, Bureau of Census, *Characteristics of the South and East Los Angeles Areas, 1965,* Current Population Reports, Technical Statistics, Series P-23, No. 18 (Washington, D.C.: Government Printing Office, 1966), Table 3.
21. U.S. Congress, Senate, Committee on Government Operations, *Federal Role in Urban Affairs, Hearings,* before the Subcommittee on Executive Reorganization of the Committee on Government Operations, Part 6, Senate, 89th Cong., 2nd sesAs., 1966, p. 1258.
22. Kenneth B. Clark, *Dark Ghetto* (New York: Harper & Row, 1965), p. 30.
23. Whitney M. Young, Jr., *To Be Equal* (New York: McGraw-Hill Book Co., 1964), pp. 144-45.
24. U.S. Department of Commerce, Bureau of the Census, *United States Census of Housing, 1960; Cleveland, Ohio, Area, Final Report* (Washington, D.C.: Government Printing Office, 1962), pp. 45-19, 45-20, 45-29.
25. Fein, p. 123.
26. Urban America, Inc., *Our people and Their Cities: Chart Book* (Washington, D.C.: Urban America, Inc.), p. 45.
27. U.S. Department of Labor, "The Negroes in the United States," Bulletin No. 1511, June 1966, pp. 39-40.
28. Kenneth A. MacDonald, "Seattle Realtors' Lobby Defeats Public Housing—Here's How," *Journal of Housing,* VII, 4 (April 1950), pp. 119-20.
29. U.S. Federal Housing Administration, *Underwriting Manual,* quoted in National Committee Against Discrimination in Housing, "How the Federal Government Builds Ghettos," (New York: National Committee Against Discrimination in Housing, 1967), p. 18.
30. *The Racial Gap,* p. 35.
31. Eunice and George Grier, "The Impact of Race on Neighborhood in the Metropolitan Setting," Address to the Washington Center for Metropolitan Studies, April 27, 1961, p. 12.
32. *New York Times,* June 15, 1967, p. A1.
33. Herbert J. Gans, "The White Exodus to Suburbia Steps Up," *New York Times Magazine,* January 7, 1968, p. 26.
34. Leella Smith, "Apartment Integration in Suburban Washington: A Survey of the Effects of Admitting Negro Tenants to Apartments Pre-

viously Closed to Them," American Friends Service Committee, Washington, D.C., 1967 (mimeographed), p. 1.
35. United States Commission on Civil Rights, *Racial Isolation in the Public Schools,* Vol. I (Washington, D.C.: Government Printing Office, 1967), p. 23.
36. *Federal Role in Urban Affairs,* Part I, pp. 73-74.
37. D. H. Perman in collaboration with Maurice Jefferies, "Pierce Street: An Urban Renewal Experience," Urban League Neighborhood Development Center, Washington, D.C., 1966 (mimeographed), pp. 5-6.
38. *Federal Role in Urban Affairs,* Part 1, p. 50.
39. Massachusetts State Advisory Committee to the U.S. Commission on Civil Rights, *The Voice of the Ghetto: Report on Two Boston Neighborhood Meetings,* 1967, p. 41.
40. *Hearing Before the United States Commission on Civil Rights, San Francisco, California, May 1-3, 1967 and Oakland, California, May 4-6, 1967,* p. 52.
41. Governor's Commission on the Los Angeles Riots, *Violence in the City—An End or a Beginning,* Los Angeles, 1965, p. 65.
42. Ibid., pp. 73-74.
43. United States Commission on Civil Rights, *A Time to Listen . . . A Time to Act: Voices from the Ghettos of the Nation's Cities,* Washington, D.C., 1967, p. 20.
44. Hobson v. Hanson, 269-F SUPP. 401 (1967), reprinted in *Congressional Record,* June 21, 1967, p. H7665-66.
45. "How the Federal Government Builds Ghettos," p. 19.
46. *Washington Post,* September 18, 1967, p. A2.
47. "How the Federal Government Builds Ghettos," pp. 24-27.
48. Ibid., p. 16.
49. Ibid.
50. *Washington Post,* November 14, 1967, p. A6.
51. U.S. Housing and Home Finance Agency, Office of the Administrator, *Our Nonwhite Population and Its Housing: The Changes Between 1950 and 1960,* Washington, D.C., 1963, p. 3.
52. "Pierce Street: An Urban Renewal Experience," p. 2.
53. *Hearing Before the United States Commission on Civil Rights, Cleveland, Ohio,* April 1-7, 1966, p. 37.
54. *A time to Listen . . . A Time to Act,* p. 16.
55. *Racial Isolation in the Public Schools,* p. 100.
56. Ibid., pp. 106, 107.
57. Ibid., p. 7.
58. Sweatt v. Painter, 339 U.S. 629 (1950), reprinted in *The Supreme Court on Racial Discrimination,* ed. by Joseph Tussman (New York: Oxford University Press, 1963), pp. 33-34.
59. Brown v. Board of Education, 347 U.S. 483 (1954), ibid., pp. 41, 42.
60. Hobson v. Hansen, pp. H7667, H7666, H7665, H7669-88.
61. U.S. Department of Health, Education, and Welfare, *Equality of Educational Opportunity,* by James S. Coleman et al., (Washington, D.C.: Government Printing Office, 1966), pp. 3, 40.
62. Kenneth B. Clark, "Social and Economic Implications of Integration in the Public Schools," Seminar on Manpower Policy and Programs, U.S. Department of Labor, Manpower Administration, Office of Manpower, Automation and Training, 1964, p. 6.

63. *Racial Isolation in the Public Schools,* p. 93.
64. *Equality of Educational Opportunity,* p. 100.
65. Hobson v. Hansen, p. H7666.
66. Jeremy Larner, "The New York School Crisis," *Dissent* (Spring 1964), reprinted in *Poverty in America,* ed. by Louis A Ferman, Joyce L. Kornbluh and Alan Haber (Ann Arbor: University of Michigan Press, 1965), p. 375.
67. *Hearing Before the United States Commission on Civil Rights, Cleveland, Ohio,* p. 289.
68. Kenneth B. Clark, "Educational Stimulation of Racially Disadvantaged Children," in *Education in Depressed Areas,* ed. by A. Harry Passow (New York: Bureau of Publications, Teachers College, Columbia University, 1963), p. 148.
69. Robert Rosenthal and Lenore Jacobson, "Self-fulfillng Prophecies in the Classroom: Teachers' Expectations as Unintended Determinant of Pupils' Intellectual Competence," Address to the American Psychological Association, Washington, D.C., September 4, 1967.
70. Robert Rosenthal and Kermit Fode, "The Effect of Experimenter Bias on the Performance of the Albino Rat," *Behavioral Science,* VIII (1963), pp. 183-89.
71. Clark, *Dark Ghetto,* p. 128.
72. U.S. Commission on Civil Rights Conference, "Equal Educational Opportunity in America's Cities: Problems and Programs for Change," Group No. D-1, The Parents, the Community and Equal Educational Opportunity, Washington, D.C., November 17, 1967, p. 13.
73. Ibid., p. 53.

Chapter 5

1. James Baldwin, "Down at the Cross: Letter from a Region in My Mind," *The Fire Next Time,* A Delta Book (New York: Dell Publishing Co., Inc., 1964), p. 111.
2. National Advisory Commission on Civil Disorders, *Report of the National Advisory Commission on Civil Disorders,* Bantam Books (New York: The New York Times Company, 1968), p. 288.
3. U.S. Congress, Senate, Committee on Government Operations. *Federal Role in Urban Affairs, Hearings,* before the Subcommittee on Executive Reorganization of the Committee on Government Operations, Part 5, Senate, 89th Cong., 2nd sess., 1966, p. 1108.
4. Educational Policies Commission, *American Education and the Search for Equal Opportunity* (Washington, D.C.: National Education Association of the United States, 1965), p. 23.
5. Carl A. Marburger, "Considerations for Educational Planning," in *Education in Depressed Areas,* ed. by A. Harry Passow (New York: Bureau of Publications, Teachers College, Columbia University, 1963), p. 308.
6. *Federal Role in Urban Affairs,* pp. 1094-95.
7. William Raspberry, "City's Infant Mortality Rate Is Alarming," *Washington Post,* December 10, 1967, p. B1.
8. George James, "Poverty as an Obstacle to Health Progress in Our Cities," *American Journal of Public Health,* LV, 11 (November, 1965), p. 1764.

9. Arthur Pearl and Frank Riessman, *New Careers for the Poor: The Nonprofessional in Human Service* (New York: Free Press; London: Collier-Macmillan Limited, 1965), pp. 55-74.
10. "Report on the D.C. Commissioners' Citizens Committee on the Eleventh Precinct of the Metropolitan Police Department," Washington, D.C., 1966 (mimeographed), p. 41.
11. President's Commission on Law Enforcement and Administration of Justice, *The Challenge of Crime in a Free Society* (Washington, D.C.: Government Printing Office, 1967), pp. 68, 98, 108-09, 118, 1x.
12. Leon ... f Work," *Wash*

Chapter

1. W. ... *3 Negro Clas* ... *Autobiog-raph* ... earst Cor-pora
2. *Hea* ... *ts,* Cleve-land
3. Ted ... " in *Race and* ... owenstein (spo ... Freedom of I ...
4. Wil ... *America* (Ne
5. Wil ... rument of the
6. Wil ... p. 82.
7. Pos
8. U.S ... rce, *Social and* ... *tates,* BLS Rep ... 3, No. 24 (W ... 11.
9. U.S ... ns, *Federal Ro* ... on Execu-tiv ... Operations, Pa

Chapte

1. Ch ... ld, Mead & Co
2. Jo ... *ok* (Engle-wo ... 420-21.
3. Jo ... *r* (Chicago: Th